About the Author

Diane Dèlos is French with a melting pot of origins: Swiss, Italian, Russian… She is passionate about travel and likes to meet others' cultures that nourish her spirituality.

And Buddha Gave Me a Son

Diane Delos

And Buddha Gave Me a Son

Olympia Publishers
London

www.olympiapublishers.com
OLYMPIA PAPERBACK EDITION

Copyright © Diane Delos 2024

The right of Diane Delos to be identified as author of
this work has been asserted in accordance with sections 77 and 78 of
the Copyright, Designs and Patents Act 1988.

All Rights Reserved

No reproduction, copy or transmission of this publication
may be made without written permission.
No paragraph of this publication may be reproduced,
copied or transmitted save with the written permission of the publisher,
or in accordance with the provisions
of the Copyright Act 1956 (as amended).

Any person who commits any unauthorised act in relation to
this publication may be liable to criminal
prosecution and civil claims for damage.

A CIP catalogue record for this title is
available from the British Library.

ISBN: 978-1-80439-877-7

This book is memoir. It reflects the author's present recollections of experiences over time. Some names and characteristics have been changed, some events have been compressed, and some dialogue has been recreated.

First Published in 2024

Olympia Publishers
Tallis House
2 Tallis Street
London
EC4Y 0AB

Printed in Great Britain

Dedication

To my son, Ngawang Jampa; to my granddaughter, Tenzin Yeshe; and to the people I love and who will recognise each other.

Acknowledgements

Thank you to my dearest friend, Nadia for encouraging me.
Thank you to my precious translator, Uma Panigrahi.

Prologue

We are driving back to Kathmandu in this car without exchanging a single word.

The road is winding and full of ruts. The bumpy journey keeps giving us jerks. I can't relax, let alone sleep.

Thoughts overwhelm me that prevent me from meditating to calm my torment and sadness.

Once again, I am leaving the one who came into my life one day without notice.

I live in Switzerland and he lives in Nepal.

Our paths have been crossing continuously since we first met in India.

I close my eyes and let the images of our life invade me with nostalgia.

Our story was perhaps written in advance, but I had no idea that it would one day materialise. Quite unlikely for me at the time to think of getting into such an incredible relationship across the seas. But our lives led us on the same path.

An invisible force enabled us to weave indestructible bonds forever.

We coped with all the hardships that came our way and that could have put a stop to this relationship.

The language barrier, the distance, the lack of contact, such few encounters… But the subconscious attraction coming from within our hearts was inevitable without our realizing what was happening.

We felt rather shy during the early stages being culturally different, or rather totally the opposite, I would say.

At the beginning, we did not dare to discover each other, being bound by our inhibitions. We lacked the words to gradually move towards an intimacy that we desired, but over the years we have managed to create bonds that today unite us for life. My memory recalls tenderly.

Physically Yours

I am fifteen years old and I am lying on my bed, casually turning the pages of a Paris Match magazine. One article catches my attention. It features Tibetan monks and hermits living in caves in the Himalayas and relates the story of the Dalai Lama and Tibet. I have never heard of either of them. I don't know why, but I plunge into reading about this subject and my imagination sweeps me over there. I envy these lamas; I would like to be in their place and be a hermit.

I am fascinated by what I have been reading and somehow by magic, I find myself with them. I let myself be lulled by these images and I like to dream of living like them. They talk about meditation, Tibetan Buddhism, the Dalai Lama, which does not mean anything to me. I have never heard of this country and this culture, but I decide that one day I will go and live there, don't ask me why. I am a very sensitive person, who sometimes likes to be alone. I am attracted by the extraordinary, the unperceivable and knowing that it is possible to escape just through the thought process seduces me. This article on Tibet really had an impact on me and touched me deeply. Time passes with this desire that is anchored in me. I think about it sometimes with emotion and keep this feeling deep inside me. I am going through a difficult period. I don't like school any more and I don't care about my life because I really don't know what I would like for myself. To be free maybe… of what? Just free to live. I am only a young teenager and a little lost like so many others.

A year goes by the best way it can and during the new term, school becomes an ordeal for me. I start skipping classes. I am in an in-between phase; I don't know what will become of me. I let myself be carried away by the present moment and don't look too much into my future. In this school, I feel rather out of place with the others, whom I still consider as immature. I only have one friend Anna, the daughter of a famous psychoanalyst. She is locked in a rigid family structure that does not let her be herself while she only dreams of flying to horizons that would not please to his parents. I notice a student who feels me more awake than the others by the noise of rumors. I learn that he makes music. I do everything to get closer to him... Lucas.

Suddenly, we discover different desires to live as one and we become friends. We talk about freedom, going out, having fun, dancing and partying. He tells me that he goes to a disco in Saint-Germain-des-Prés on Saturday nights. How I would love to experience this nightlife!

I am just celebrating my sixteenth birthday and my parents, who are broad minded and easy going, let me go out on weekends. I'm so lucky: they trust me completely. They allow me to venture out of the family cocoon, which is still rare for a girl of my age.

As a result, I meet my classmate in the disco where he goes on Saturday nights. I am entering into a new life that has nothing to do with the one before.

We don't do anything wrong, just dance and live without constraints. What a sweet feeling it is to twirl and sway on the dance floor and feel so light!

The other students, when they hear that we had gone out at night, think we have gone berserk and ask us lots of questions.

We become idols and they dream of being in our place.

My friend Anna is jealous of my freedom but especially of my closeness with Lucas, she is so in love of him… in secret. She constantly asks me to tell her about my escapades and live them through.

We are outsiders for them. My friend, a handsome dark-haired boy of Italian descent, is always dressed in smooth velvet pants, very dandy. As for me, I'm a real blonde, diaphanous but above all tall for my age, which does not make me go unnoticed. I like to dress in long bohemian dresses with an Indian scarf in my hair, in high fashion during that era.

We have a bevy of fans around us who admire us, who want to know in detail what we are up to, and there is the second lot, a bunch of "holier-than-thou" grumblers whom we find detestable, scowling at us disapprovingly from afar, but I imagine secretly envious and at the same time disdainful.

In high school, I start skipping more and more classes, starting with one morning then a whole day and finally upgrading to two months.

I leave each morning and take the bus to Paris. I discover my city by wandering in the streets while dreaming of an uncertain future. I don't know how I go about it, but I still manage to hide the truth from my unsuspecting parents.

I do not feel guilty about this situation. I am like in a dream and do not want to wake me up.

One day, by a stroke of luck, I bump into the postman delivering the mail! I intercept a letter from the school. I open it anxiously. They want to know the reason for my absences. I am panic stricken, the truth will be disclosed… what a disaster!

Then a devilish idea comes into me. My brother is a medical student and an intern in the hospital in psychiatry. He has access to prescriptions from the department where he works. I sneak in there, grab hold of one of the blank forms and fill out the certificate to myself explaining that I am undergoing a nervous breakdown.

How on earth could I ever do such a thing? I'm still wondering till today!

And then as predicted, the principal of the high school calls us up to enquire about my condition.

My mother is stunned and doesn't know what to say.

That same evening, a family meeting is held during which I go through a tough ordeal.

But why? What was to become of me? What have I done?

You are a liar, we don't trust you any more.

I don't know what to say. I just explain that I don't want to go to school any more. That I don't feel good there. That I have nothing to do there any more.

My parents want to hear nothing of it.

It was decided that I would go straight back to school the following day and that I would complete my education.

I reach the school where I report to the principal.

Sitting behind his desk, he greets me with a blank and severe face, reminiscent of a commissioner in a black and white film played by an amateurish actor. This ghastly looking man, who is tall with an emaciated face, sweating all over, and could be quite scary to look at, leaves me completely indifferent.

I put myself in a protective shield and I don't hear a word of what he is saying. His lecture sounds as if it came straight out of a third-grade soap opera that falls like water on a duck's feathers on me.

I hang my head down without revealing any emotions.

Maybe he would have wanted me to cry or apologise, but I don't say anything and just nod at his scolding, without the slightest regret inside me. He curtly sends me back to class.

The morning drags on painfully, I don't understand anything about the course going on, having missed so many days. I look out the window just as dunces do and count the minutes until the end of this ordeal.

Slowly time leads me towards the lunch break. Its noon and the bell rings. Free, finally I am "free".

I rush outside to take a deep breath of fresh air. I need to breathe, to fill my lungs with oxygen. I'm not interested in studying any more, I'm a stranger in this school. I've really disconnected myself.

On my way home, I think about my life, about school, and decide that as far as I'm concerned, I'm really not cut out for studies.

I can't, I don't want to, I don't feel like going on like this any more. My school-going days are over.

At home, my mother asks me how the morning went. I burst into tears and huddle in her arms. I suffocate; I am after all still a child.

I explain to her in my own words, between two sobs, what I feel, that I don't think I can make it to the end and that it would be better if I started working.

She can't quite figure out what's wrong but tells me that she only wants my happiness, that we will see with my father in the evening at dinner.

She never decides on her own. I am afraid of my father's reaction.

When he arrives in the evening from work, my mother explains the situation to him.

He is rather bewildered about my decision. He looks sad but what can I do? I am myself distraught at having to face this hurricane that I have just triggered off.

He tries to convince me with his arguments, those of a father worried about his daughter's future, which is perfectly justified and makes sense, but I have made up my mind.

I explain my plans to him, which I must admit are not clear to me either, because I don't know myself the deep reasons. I rather mumble nonsense, I would rather say.

He sees me distraught, sad but determined. He asks me to think about it during the night and that we would discuss it the next day. But for me:

The die is cast.

The next day, I confirm my decision. My father, with a blank face, tries again to dissuade me but I remain firm and refuse all suggestions.

He then asks me coldly not to sit at home doing nothing; I must find a job quickly because he does not want to see me idle.

Not that easy finding a job when you don't have any qualifications, so how do I go about it and where do I go?

My mother has an idea and explains it to me because she sees me looking so lost.

Our neighbour, who works in a very famous photo lab, could maybe help me because she likes me a lot.

I find it's an excellent idea and I decide to go to visit her as soon as the evening comes.

The day passes quietly, it is the first time that the agenda of my life is empty, no more school, just the uncertainty of the next day.

I must admit that it's not bad doing nothing and just letting myself go.

I once again think about my life until now and somehow Tibet automatically comes back to mind, I don't know why.

Now that I'm on stand-by, maybe I could go there to immerse myself in the culture and finally discover these hermit monks.

I could be a nun, but in the article, they were talking about monks, not nuns. Do Buddhist nuns also exist?

I thus dream of a future that may be utopian but could one day become reality who knows.

The hours simply drag on when one does nothing. I can hardly wait for the evening to go across to this dear neighbour and talk to her.

After dinner, impatient, I ring her doorbell shyly. Odette is a divorced woman with two grown up children now. She is dynamic and manages her life with rigor. She devotes her entire life to her work in a photo lab well known among professionals. She has gained the trust of her entire team, which is a bit like her family.

She listens carefully to me while I am explaining to her about my leaving school and that I don't quite know what to do but that I promised my parents to find a job.

She scolds me and tells me that school is important, well, the sort of lecture an adult would give to a teenager who has thrown up everything overnight. She smiles at me and tells me that she will see what she can do.

She'll have a word with her team tomorrow and let me know as soon as she has any news.

She is a serious person whom I can count on. So I am full of hope. I thank her and go back to tell my parents about our discussion.

They are themselves delighted and I can see from the twinkle in their eyes that they are a little more reassured about my future.

Days go by. I have no news. I don't dare to knock and ask her whether she has any news.

The weekend arrives, still nothing. I start to despair, my mother pushes me to go and see her, but I don't want to; I am a proud person and don't like going begging to people.

It's Saturday when the doorbell rings: it's her. I am impatient and nervous. My parents offer her a drink and we do some light talk as if nothing had happened, just about the rain and the sun. I start having my doubts about a job perspective when she herself brings up the subject. She spoke to the big boss who offered me a job as a student for two months, and then they'll see how things go.

Two months. I'm rather doubtful, but it's true that I have no qualifications and that it was I who chose this situation, so I shouldn't have any grudges. My parents are happy.

They say that I will start the following Monday.

A new adventure starts for me. I creep into the business world through the back-door.

I get up early that morning but still a bit anxious. *What am I going to do once I join there? What will the job consist of? Will the colleagues be nice? Will I be accepted?*

With all these questions in mind, I set off on my great journey. Though autumn is nearing its end and winter is just round the corner, a beautiful sun guides me through my way and brightens my hopes. *Do I take it as an auspicious sign?*

My first day after joining passes by smoothly. Odette, my neighbour, introduces me to her team of two female office workers who give me a warm welcome.

I am asked to do some filing of customers' records, nothing extraordinary. I wonder if I've been hired just to get out of the mess I put myself into and to have some enjoyment. I have the impression that they don't really need me, but well…

At lunchtime, my two colleagues suggest that I join them for lunch at the local bistro/café. Frankly, I must admit that I didn't think at all about the practical conveniences like meals or how long it would take me to get to work, because the lab is at the other end of Paris.

The meal is frugal and consists of a sandwich, which is quite a contrast as compared to mummy's wholesome home-made meals.

The girls chat as if we've known each other for a long time. I tell them about my life, why I am here.

They tell me that I was right in quitting school if I didn't feel like it. They are simple and kind. They are in their thirties and already have families, having been married for several years. I don't envy them. I don't yearn for a life like theirs.

The afternoon is also spent quietly, putting things in place.

When I get home, my mother overwhelms me with questions, and then, in the evening it's my father's turn.

What did I do? How was the atmosphere at the workplace like?

I answer enthusiastically, a little proud of myself. I tell them about this first day. The next day, I'm happy to go back to work.

In the afternoon, a famous photographer visits the lab and asks us to develop some shots he had just done for a lingerie brand.

Odette knows everyone and highly reputed in her profession. She's been working there for years, has all the credit and actually runs the company.

The photographer is fully aware of this and goes directly to her. She calls me to introduce me to him, explaining my situation. He doesn't seem friendly and talks nervously without a pause. I guess he is in his fifties and is already greying.

I am embarrassed, and even more so by the way he looks at me, strangely, examining me from head to toe.

I think to myself:

What has overcome him that he is staring at me that way, almost undressing me with his eyes?

The girls I work with laugh.

- Well! well, you interest Robert.
- Ah! well, and in what sense can I be of any interest to him?
- You're his type.
- His type? But he's old!
- Not for what you are thinking, for the photos.
- It's not for nothing that Odette introduced you to him.
- I really don't understand anything of what's going on.

The week passes quite quickly. I rather like this job, which isn't that complicated after all. A disciplined routine follows, and my days are now punctuated similar to the notations on a sheet of music, that is underground subway-work-underground subway-sleep.

The following Monday morning, Odette asks me to join her at her office.
- Do you remember, Robert, the photographer?
- The one who persisted in staring at me last week?
- Yes, him. He would like to take some test photos with you.
- But what for?
- For fashion or advertising photos, you have the looks. You're tall, thin, pretty and blonde. He'd like to see how you would come out on a photo.
- Are you sure?
- Of course I am, so will you take it or leave it?
- Yes, I'd like to, but I think I have to consult my parents first.
- Sure, ask them and let me know.

By the time evening comes, I'm jumping for joy, terribly excited about the idea that a photographer has noticed me and wants to make me a model, well maybe.

My parents calm down my joy and once again I get the usual precautionary lecture.

"Is this a job? Who is he? Is he serious? Don't get too excited, it's only a trial period."

In other words, it means that they accept what I'm doing and have given me the freedom to choose my way.

Once Odette gets my parents' non-objection, she telephones the photographer to tell him that it's confirmed. He tells her rather coldly that he'll call to fix an appointment for me when he has a moment.

My excitement collapses like a pin-pricked balloon, I who already visualised myself as the number one model on the catwalk, this comes to me like a slap on the face. Could he have forgotten me already?

There's no point in brooding about it any more, I just leave it at the corner of my mind. At the office, nobody brings up the subject any more, which is what I prefer.

I carry on with my work with less enthusiasm but still satisfied in my job.

A fortnight later, I think I hear a familiar voice coming from Odette's office that I'm sure I can recognise. Yes, it's him, I'm sure of it! I go to find an excuse to see him, but before I can react, he appears in front of me as if nothing had happened.
- Hello Diane, are you still willing to consider doing those test shots?

I blush and am barely able to stammer:
- Yes Monsieur.
- Oh! Please call me Robert, in our business we call each other by our first names.
- "All right," I say in a whisper.

I'll meet you next Monday at my studio on rue Marbeuf, at three o'clock. Come with a clean scrubbed face, without make-up and with your hair washed. I've arranged with Odette for you to be free that day.
- I'll be there without fail.
- See you next week, Diane!
- Yes Mons... Robert.

My colleagues giggle. When he leaves, they surround me, chuckling and giggling in chorus:
- That's great, you'll see, you'll be a thundering success in the modeling business.

I feel as if I'm floating in some heavenly cloud of fluffy pink cotton.

Finally, Robert changes the scheduled date and place of the appointment, but only by two days.

On D-day, I find myself in a photo studio at Les Halles, in the heart of the capital, the belly of Paris as Emile Zola so aptly wrote. Robert is waiting for me, accompanied by a pretty girl who doesn't seem to me to be a model, being too short.

- Hi Diane, let me introduce you to Chantal, my make-up artist and hairdresser, who will be taking care of you for this photo shoot.

Now I understand why Robert asked me to come without any make-up and with clean hair.

Rather awkwardly, I greet Chantal in a whisper.

- "Come along with me," she says and leads me to the back of the studio where there is a table and a mirror with an array of make-up products, brushes and creams.

It's enough to transform an ordinary person in no time at all.

- So here we are, Robert wants me to turn your baby face into a sexy Lolita.

I'm flabbergasted, "baby face", "Lolita", terms I hadn't ever heard before. Lolita, of course, I know the name, which I think comes from Nabokov's book, but baby face?

I enter the life of a model and her very special world.

An hour later, amidst the fragrances of blushers, unknown perfumes and that unique touch of something that one can only imagine in a movie studio, I am transformed, with an undone hair bun à la Brigitte Bardot, long-lasting eye make-up, a pouting cherry mouth.

I don't recognise myself one bit and I can't stop looking at myself in the mirror.

I catch myself saying:

- Chantal, you are a fairy. I am beautiful. I'm not me any more.
- Well, you see, that's what my job is: to transform, to beautify, to mould someone who has potential, to be at the photographer's service.

And make a beautiful girl like you into a magazine cover-girl.

Robert arrives and nods approvingly when he sees me.

- Perfect Chantal, that's what I wanted, a real Lolita!
- Dress her in the gypsy dress with the accessories that go with it.

We'll go outdoors for the first shots. I'd love to see people's reactions.

Hearing this makes me blush and panic at the thought of showing my face to others.

- Robert, are you sure I can do this?
- Don't worry little one, just let yourself go and think you're playing a part.

This advice accompanied me throughout my career and it really came in handy when I had to deal with a photographer who didn't know his job and didn't know how to direct.

The first outfit is a long muslin dress, in chic hippie style. I am made to wear rows of tangled necklaces, flashy bracelets and 10 cm high shoes, and as if I wasn't tall enough, my heights easily shoots up to 1 metre 87cm.

I can't recognise myself, I believe I look beautiful, but I see a stranger before me… In fact, that's what Robert wanted, for me to be someone else, to play a role.

I understood it and I'm now ready to perform.

Robert goes out first, looking for a suitable spot in front of the studio to photograph me. He decides that it should be by the telephone booth.

He tells me to go inside and pretend to make a phone call while striking sexy poses.

I do so, and people start getting closer to the scene, wondering what's going on and who we're photographing.

I hesitatingly start posing, feeling really self-conscious in front of the crowd that has meanwhile gathered around the place. I am disturbed to be the centre of attraction.

Robert comes up to my ear and talks to me.

- You're alone, you're phoning your guy you're in love with, go on, forget everything, just let go of yourself and get into your character. He's older than you and you are taking advantage of this difference.

I take a deep breath and gradually put myself in the role of an enticing and seductive woman in love, something that I never dreamt of being but that I now imagine myself to be.

- Well, that's how it is, move your hair, open your mouth, great!

I hear whispers in the audience but I don't understand what is being said.

I feel I'm getting swept off my feet and I like it.

After an hour, we stop and Robert tells Chantal to change my look for the studio shots.

She undoes everything that had been done earlier to transform me into a prim and proper school girl.

Nude make-up, straightened hair.

Everyone starts giggling, as now we're doing just the opposite.

After the sexy and provocative chic hippie look, I'm turned into a naive goody and we laugh even more when I practice acting innocent.

It's really fun and I'm feeling more and more at ease.

I'm dressed like a schoolgirl, with a pleated skirt, a baby-collar blouse and flat ballerina shoes.

The session begins.

- This time you're an innocent kid, Robert tells me.

We're amongst ourselves in the studio, and I'm thoroughly enjoying myself, as there is no one to look at us or to scrutinize me up and down.

I play the pure, innocent girl he wants me to be which is in fact what I actually am. He gives me a lollipop to play with. I understand much later that these photos had a hidden eroticism about them, but at that time I was just a kid.

What a mischievous rascal this Robert was!

We end with a series of portraits for me taken in a hurry. I'm sitting on a footstool and he turns around me. I just have to look at the lens. I don't know what the result will be as it's nothing like the previous two sessions.

I'm eager to see the results, bubbling with euphoria and excitement. My life has turned into a real fairy tale.

Did they bend over my cradle without my knowing it, or is Buddha guiding me down this path to make me understand something?

It was many years later that I got the answer.

In the meantime, I set forth to go back home to relate this beautiful dream and share it with my family.

My mother, before my father arrives, bombards me with

questions, and is as excited as I am. I tell her about the whole day, point by point, the make-up artist, the transformations, the people outside looking at me, in short, this whole daydream.

My father is less enthusiastic about my story and mumbles between his teeth what he is used to saying, "Yeah well, it's not a job."

It only lasts for a while; you won't learn anything.

But you can't change him, that's typically his character, always worrying about me and wanting me to succeed in life. I understand him deep down, but what he hopes for me is far from what I hope for myself.

At work, everyone asks me how the session went, and absolutely overjoyed, I take great pride in excitedly relating every detail with precision, my impressions, my feelings, and at the same time reliving each moment again with emotion.

Again, I have no news from Robert, a deadly silence for me.

I don't dare to talk about it and remain silent, and my colleagues, seeing me looking so glum, do not bring up the subject. I ask myself many questions about myself and my future.

Then, just as it happened the first time, I hear Robert's voice coming from the neighbouring office room. I don't dare go in there, I'm petrified. What should I do? I pretend to work, but my mind is elsewhere.

He pokes his head out from the doorway. There she is… the model, the one who will make it big?

My colleagues shout :
- Come on, she's waiting for you.

- Well, here are the results of that day's photo shoot.

And he dumps about fifteen photos on the table.

- Not bad at all, Mademoiselle, he says to me.

I hardly dare to glance at them, and so do my colleagues.

- Come on, girls, take a serious look, don't be so silly just gaping at us, yells Robert.

I can't believe my eyes, but above all I don't recognise myself. I see someone other than myself, beautiful and with a character.

I hear "ohs", "ahs", "how beautiful you are", "it's terrific Laure".

- "So, my little one," says Robert, this is only the beginning.

Tomorrow you have an appointment at Models' Agency, you'll meet Gérald, who is a booker, and he'll tell you what he thinks about this. I've spoken to him about you, he can't wait to see you with your photos.

He's a renowned professional, his judgement and flair are infallible but above all he knows the entire fashion and media world of Paris.

All of a sudden, everything goes too fast, my head spins, I'm flabbergasted and can't pronounce a single word, nor can I express my delight.

- Don't be afraid, little one, just be natural, believe in yourself and trust in life. If it works, it's your destiny.

And my destiny is on its way.

The next day, Odette gives me the day off to go to the agency on Avenue Victor Hugo, near the Étoile, which is not so far from the offices where I work.

Gérald receives me straight away, a nice chap, but I notice that he is examining me from head to toe as if nothing had happened.

I'm embarrassed, I'm feeling hot and I start feeling rather sick at the smell floating in the air, an unfamiliar oriental perfume, which is in fact patchouli. My throat itches and I cough. He looks up at me.

- So its Robert who discovered you... You know he's a great photographer!
- Yes, I do.
- Show me your photos, so that I can see how you come out.

He takes them, spreads them out in front of him, then there is a total silence.

He calls a colleague of his who is also a booker.

- Samantha, come and take a look at this.

He shows her the photos.

She is silent and utters onomatopoeia like: *hum hum,* "yeah", "oh yes", *poh poh poh.*

A very strange language for me.

- "So?" asks Gerald.

And she says only one word:

- Great!

And she leaves without saying anything more or even looking at me. Gerald sighs heavily.

In my head I say to myself:

It's over, he doesn't like me, he doesn't think I'm anything special.

Suddenly I'm completely frozen, as if paralysed. The earlier sensation of heat now gives way to a freezing shudder all over.

- Diane, I've studied your photos and... You're going to

be part of my team, I'll look after you personally. Robert judged correctly, you do have a future.

And thus, a new life begins for me.

*

Being a model isn't as simple as one thinks, actually. It's not just about smiling or pleasing clients and photographers. There's all the start-up work and preparation that needs to be done before getting hired and walking in front of the camera or on the catwalk.

Every day, Gérald, who has now taken complete charge over me, fixes my appointments or castings.

I have to appear before a photographer, an advertising agency, a magazine, a fashion designer, a fashion boutique, etc. I have to come dressed in a neutral outfit, wear high heels when I arrive but during the day I prefer to wear flat heels, which is far more comfortable when getting in and out of subways and walking from one end of picture book to show!

Gerald has started sending me to several photographers to create my portfolio which depicts me in different styles. Of course, Robert's photos are also in there.

Then a choice is made to make a composite which is the business card of models.

Several full-length portrait photos, my name, the agency's name and my measurements make up this one, which I always leave behind so that I am remembered.

Once everything is put in place, my life as a model can begin and, spins off at one go. Gerald fills in my diary with appointments. He wants me to get recognised quickly. Some days are sluggish, then everything happens at the same time and it's a real race.

Of course, I'm not the only one to perform and you can feel a wave of jealousy during these castings' sessions, each candidate desperately striving to make it to the top. We turn up our noses and glare distastefully at each other trying hard to find some fault in our rivals.

Most of them are foreigners and an unintelligible gibberish of languages ranging from English to Swedish and passing on to German can be heard, in other words, a real cosmopolitan world tour.

I didn't experience the follies of the late eighties and the supermodels that era had produced, but I can only imagine that they must have had a tough time during the castings to bag the top position.

I don't know if I would have been able to cope in that jungle where you had to cut each other's throat and at the same time be hypocritical towards everyone.

So, in my time, it's still fun because there's no pressure to be the best.

Swedish and American women are currently in vogue. Despite the competitive environment, I still make friends in this hybrid multicultural group namely with Birgit, a Danish girl.

We meet at the castings a few times and afterwards, depending on our schedule, we go for a coffee at Le Flore, in Saint-Germain-des-Prés.

I am thus able to improve my English by mixing with so many different nationalities, because none of them speak French and Shakespeare's language becomes our official language of communication.

What I learnt at school comes back to me, I feel I'm managing quite well, and I'm really proud of it.

My first casting is for a not particularly well-known brand of ready-to-wear clothes but which is well established in the Sentier, the wholesale clothing district.

They want photos of a girl for their catalogue of ready-mades at a garment's exhibition.

I must admit that upon setting foot in the shop I am rather overawed, especially as I was not expecting a simple shop so far from the world of haute couture and its plush saloons.

I follow all the instructions given to me in detail, and show up in high heels, with my hair tied back in a pony tail, and wearing jeans and an inconspicuous T-shirt and with light, neutral make-up.

The manager, a man in his thirties and of Mediterranean descent, receives me kindly and tells me what he wants while looking at my book.

He wants the person he chooses to do the photos and also the fashion shows at the ready-made trade fair that will soon take place at the Porte de Versailles.

- "Is this possible for you?" he asks me without looking up from my book.

- "Yes," I answer, not having the remotest idea of what knowing what the consequences will be.

- Well! Diane, I have to meet other models so I'll give my answer to Gerald afterwards.

- So, maybe I'll see you soon, I say, not finding any other words.

I walk out drained out and puzzled. Is this what this job is all about? To be a nonentity or a person whom people look right into without knowing who she is?

In the evening, at home, I talk about my first appointment and as usual, my father mumbles from behind his beard:

- What a nonsensical bunch of models.

Two days later, I'm at the agency to follow-up with Gérald on what was agreed upon, and he asks me how the meeting I had at the Sentier went.

- I don't know, he told me he had to see other girls, he was nice but nothing more. I don't know what will be the final decision.
- Well! darling, you're hired. First casting, first contract, well done.
- Well! as far as the catalogue shots are concerned, no problem, but the ready-to-wear show, that's to be seen because it's tiring and I don't know if you're ready to go for it, but it's the deal, the catalogue and the show.

Let me explain.

You have to parade on his stand for his clients and also on the central podium four times a day. But it pays well and there's always a first start for everything, isn't it?

If you accept the proposal, which I advise you to do, you will need to get a power of attorney signed by your parents because you are a still a minor. This will be used to accept all future contracts until you come of age.

And that's how it all began... my real life as a model.

I must admit that all goes off perfectly well since I started this career. I am disciplined, obedient, docile, I am learning and I like learning.

Just a week after I'm hired for the fashion catalogue, I'm to start the photo shoot.

What a disappointment! It had nothing to do with Robert, the photographer who discovered me.

I have to do my own make-up and have my hair in a bun. Those days, it was quite common to have models hired by a small studio do their own make-up without the help of a professional.

Nowadays, this would be something unthinkable, as make-up and hair are done by professionals. A stylist chooses the clothes, the accessories... But for me, it was the beginning of the eighties, before the arrival of the famous models-turned-celebrities receiving colossal fees.

I am quite satisfied with my small fees that allow me to live comfortably. Sometimes it happens that I earn more than my father's monthly salary. I am free and happy.

The photographer is a kind man, and though far from being a top professional from what I gather, nevertheless does his job well. The clothes I am made to wear are simple.

A lot of jersey jumpers, flowing dresses also made of jersey material, nothing special. All the shots are taken in his studio against a white background without any assistant, just the two of us.

In three hours, everything is made ready for the catalogue. All that remains is my participation in the ready-to-wear show for this range of clothes next month and I think it will far from relaxing.

In the meantime, I've been selected for a brand of cleansing gel for teenagers with sensitive skin and a lightening chamomile-based shampoo.

Nothing spectacular, but makes me earn a living, it's very well paid and my face will start appearing in magazines when the ads will be published.

Here I am, off to the famous ready-to-wear show. I arrive early because I'm afraid of being late on this first day.

I go to the stand; the director is already there. I was right in arriving in advance. He explains what is expected of me, nothing exciting but that's how it is.

When customers visit the stand, I start presenting their clothing collection by parading under inadequate lighting. They call it a booth model and for me I say coat rack model, because I don't exist.

All that I am required to do is to give emphasis to the clothes I'm wearing. Between two presentations to future buyers, I am just required to smile dumbly and look beautiful like a caked-up doll.

Four times a day, I parade on the central catwalk with other models, men and women, presenting clothes of different brands at the event. I rather like it because it's a change from the stand where I'm confined to just sitting there and waiting.

At the end of the day, I'm totally exhausted, but that's part of learning the job through the back door and I can't say anything except to Gerald.

- Never again! I say to my booker.
- I warned you, my little chick, but this is your first stepping stone.

I realise that I'm starting to throw little tantrums whereas hundreds of girls would have dreamt of being in my place doing this show.

- I'm sorry, but this is not what I had expected. Waiting for clients to come in and just dress up for them is not very exciting.
- I agree with you, Diane, but you're just making your debut and it's incredible how much you're already in demand for a beginner.

Incidentally, I also wanted to give you the news that you've been hired for a swimming suit photo shoot in Greece for the catalogue of a renowned brand and here's the icing on the cake: it's going to be with Robert. Isn't that wonderful, to be in Greece, with Robert who is somewhat your godfather in this field, and that too for a famous catalogue?
- Oh! I can hardly believe it! And when are we going?
- I don't know yet, but it's getting finalized. You'll fly to Athens a few days beforehand with part of the team to start the preparations, then proceed to Mykonos, the mythical island. Robert wants you to arrive there tan-free with an alabaster skin, because the photos will be based on a Greek mythological theme set in natural surroundings.
- You're lucky he took you under his wing. You'll see what a famous model he's going to make of you!
- I'm dreaming, I'm dreaming Gerald, tell me I'm dreaming!
- No, you're not! You're wide awake, but see that you don't get your fingers burnt. Keep your feet on the ground, don't get carried away and remember, it's all artificial, time goes by quickly and others «Diane» will arrive the market.

He's right, but for now, I want to make the most of it.

*

Through the castings, my visits to the agency, or among certain clients and professionals, I gradually start building up a network of acquaintances.

I can't really call these people friends, but we are on the same wavelength, as all of us are working as models.

We like to see each other to discuss about our careers and especially to share the latest gossip in our field.

One of them, a male model whom I met when posing for a furrier, is very friendly towards me. Both of us have become ambassadors of the same brand of fur coats.

The client believes we share an irresistible chemistry as a couple helps sell the brand. He goes to the extent of renewing our contract for the following year.

Nicolas and I immediately share the same vibes and we enjoy pretending to be in love all huddled up under our fur coats.

He makes a good living from this job. We often see him in magazines or in advertisements. He is very successful and in great demand, he has a strong hold in business.

He is recognizable with his Hungarian prince look, his original native country. Elegant, sporty, very tall and stylish are the words that come to mind to describe him.

It's strange to date someone whose face is seen everywhere on ads and tabloids... But to me he's real and he's my friend. Since I was hired, we often talk on the phone and I must admit that I like talking to him.

One evening, he invites me to the Alcazar, which is a hot spot at Saint-Germain-des-Prés where everybody who is anybody in Paris rushes to. It's a music-hall with a cabaret show hosted by the dynamic and one and only Jean-Marc Rivière.

Nicolas knows the captain of the dancers, an Englishwoman,

Mary. I make out vaguely that they had had a brief relationship at one time. She provides us with tickets to the show.

I'm really excited to go there with Nicolas and to discover this place I've heard so much about.

When evening draws near, we go for dinner to a small restaurant near Odéon, not far from the cabaret.

The dinner goes off very well, we talk about everything and nothing, we laugh stupidly like children, our conversation moves on without any moments of silence, we always have something to say.

I probably attribute this to the wine, but I feel like I've known him since ages. People look at us with a friendly smile and assume we are lovers.

The waiter abruptly interrupts us by enquiring whether we are stars because our faces are not unknown to him.

Nicolas, laughing, tells him that we are not famous but that our faces are, because we are models.

- But yes, now I can visualise you! You, Mademoiselle, are that face cream and you, Sir, are the image posing before that sports car…

Can I have your autographs please?

We are surprised by this sudden shot into stardom, because we are nobody, but we comply with pleasure.

In a flash of a second, the news spreads all over the restaurant and everyone is now staring at us; fortunately, it's time to leave because it's getting rather awkward.

I understand the stars who dare not venture out of their homes. It's a trap to be a celebrity.

It's only a hundred metres away to the Alcazar, I'm a bit tipsy and intoxicated by everything that's going on.

As I enter, I am struck by the atmosphere inside. People are finishing their meal amidst the outrageous clinking and clanking of cutlery and voices, the waiters approach them and greet them in a familiar way as if they were friends.

It's the first time I've been to this kind of place and I'm intimidated.

I cling on to Nicolas who takes my hand to guide me through the dimly lit hall.

- Come on, let's go upstairs to the bar.

I feel like a little girl in Alice's Wonderland with her Prince Charming by her side.

*

We are seated at a table and Mary, the dancer, comes to greet us.
- Nicolas, darling, how are you?
- Fine, darling, this is Diane, a model friend of mine.
- Good evening, Diane, you are very beautiful, Nicolas has very good taste.

I stammer a lot of nonsense like a dumb idiot.
- The show is about to start, I have to go on stage but will see you afterwards, my darlings.

When she leaves, I am speechless and don't know what to say.

Your girlfriend is nice.

Nicolas doesn't answer me, he just smiles.

All of a sudden, a Spanish music is heard, the waiters downstairs start rushing back and forth and then there is a pin drop silence. Again we hear loud and lively music, then a man jumps up on stage.
- It is Jean-Marie Rivière, the showman and director.

Totally dazzled and awe-struck, I turn to Nicolas, but words don't come to my mouth, I feel as if I am spellbound, fascinated.

The show begins. I am stunned by what I see, magnificent, I love it, I adore it.

Nicolas explains to me as we go along what is happening on stage because it is not common.

- You see that girl with the buxom bosom that Jean-Marie introduced as a fireman? Well, she is a man, or rather a transvestite. In fact, she lives as a woman all the time.

I'm amazed, women are men, men are effeminate, everything is topsy turvy, out of this world, and I like that a lot. In fact, this is similar to modelling, we are in an artificial world out of touch with reality.

As the show progresses, Nicolas gets closer to me, touches my arm, whispers his comments in my ear and when the lights go out, he kisses me.

How wonderful it feels! And I think that's what I wanted from him. It's the first time I've really kissed a boy, and the feeling puts me into a weird, euphoric state.

Other items follow one after the other: a more-than-real Josephine Baker, Marlene Dietrich parodied in a scene from the film Agent X 27, a wild French cancan and a memorable finale for me with the whole cast singing and dancing.

Every time the lights are dimmed, our lips touch each other arousing a burning desire in utmost silence.

Mary discreetly makes signs to us when she is on stage and we smile back and wave.

I am floating on some heavenly cloud. I discover Parisian nightlife, the most fashionable show, a man who feels something that cannot be described towards me, strange sensations I never imagined having before, and emotions that were totally unknown to me till now.

I am becoming an adult but I am not yet a woman. *Will Nicolas make me a woman?*

The finale of the show finishes me off, balloons start flying, the entire cast appears on stage, singing and dancing. The waiters take part in the show, Jean-Marie Rivière lets himself go completely. He did a commendable job as a master of ceremonies.

The curtain falls, the applause stops.

The music is still ringing in my ears, my eyes are dazzled by the limelights and Nicolas' kisses have set ablaze my lips.

Mary joins us later after removing her stage make-up, and she no longer has the halo of an artist, she is just another ordinary woman.

On the other hand, I see Romy Haag, the transvestite, who is adorned with this veil of exacerbated but real femininity.

She is wearing light made up and looks more feminine than a woman. Unimaginable! How is this possible?

Jean-Marie Rivière had introduced her as an ex-fireman of Dutch origin. I can't remember exactly the story he wove around her to surprise everybody when she would come on stage, but it really created a sensation.

People expect to see some ludicrous travesty, and they see a goddess adorned in a mysterious halo.

One is not born a woman, one becomes one, as Simone de Beauvoir said in her book The Second Sex.

Romy Haag is the perfect illustration of this quote.

Mary suggests we go and take a bite somewhere, but Nicolas refuses.

- It's late and Diane has to go home.

I would have loved this beautiful evening to go on, I have

never experienced this before, to be with a man I desire and who is so considerate.

Maybe he thinks I'm too young, but I don't dare tell him that I'd like to spend the night with him and go through it all.

Outside, he hails a taxi and we get into a silence that speaks volumes. I remain silent for fear of breaking this dream; he says nothing and even seems rather worried.

- We will drop the young lady.

He gives my address mechanically.

It's such a pity that I won't be spending the night with him!

The next day, my mother comes to wake me up.

- Diane, it's Nicolas on the phone, it's already noon but I didn't dare wake you up because you came home late and I knew you had nothing to do today. Do you want to talk to him?

- Yes, Mummy, please pass me the phone.

I'm suddenly fully awake and excited to hear his voice.

- Hello, Nicholas? Thank you for such a wonderful evening.

- You're welcome, Diane, I wanted to apologise for kissing you, you're so young and I wouldn't want you to think that I wanted to take advantage of you because you're a model and in our circle we don't have such barriers. I respect you, Diane.

- Oh Nicolas, but it was magical, the evening, the show, you, and…

I whisper:

- …your kisses.

- Please Diane, just forget all that happened and think of your career first. I have to go now, a big hug to you and I'll call you soon.

He hangs up, without giving me the time neither to reply back nor to tell him my feelings.

I don't understand why, but since his last phone call I haven't heard from him. I am heartbroken. Infatuated and love-struck, all my thoughts are focused on him and are constantly hovering in my mind. Fortunately, I am involved in castings and the preparation of this trip to Greece, but in the end, I don't want to go there any more.

I would like to remain in Paris and meet Nicolas; I think I am in love. I've never experienced this before.
Totally engrossed in Nicolas, I dream about him all the time, my heart beats in excitement and makes me breathless when unknown physical emotions within me that I have never felt before make my senses tingle.
I am kept busy thanks to Gerald, who takes wonderful care of me. I'm not at home very often, which is much better in my current state of mind, as it makes me forget my incessant worries.

One evening when I get home, the phone starts ringing just as I am opening the door.
My heart is pounding, maybe it's him?
- "Diane, is that you? Hurry up and come here, there's a call for you," my mother yells from the living room.
I get to the phone, totally out of breath.
- Hello?
There is a total silence across the line.
- Diane, it's Nicolas. Would you like to have dinner with me tonight?
I know it's at the last minute, but I need to see you, to talk to

you.

Without hesitation, I answer:
- Yes, with pleasure, where shall we meet?
- The same restaurant as the other night, in Saint-Germain.
- Nicolas, don't you want to go somewhere else? We are familiar faces over there and they won't leave us in peace.
- You're right. So I'll come to pick you up and we'll decide. See you in half an hour downstairs in front of your home.
- Good, see you.
- Mum I'm going out again, Nicolas is picking me up to go to a party with models, it's for my work.

I don't know why I'm lying, maybe I want to hide the fact that I'm blossoming into a young woman and have my own secrets.

I've never talked about sex with my mother, it's not done. My parents are open-minded but we don't talk about these things in life.

Though they allow me to go out and to work, but I always have to give them a feedback about what I'm doing. They trust me but always want to know where I am.

Before Nicolas, I never had any fling or crush on anybody, but in this case it's my first relationship that I want to cherish without sharing it, not even with my mother.

I hurriedly take a shower, change my clothes and decide not to wear make-up. In twenty minutes I'm ready.

Ten minutes later, I'm downstairs.

A motorbike storms in and pulls up in front of me. The rider takes off his helmet and Nicolas' face appears like a fashion shot. He is handsome and sexy.
- Oh Nicolas, you have a motorbike!
- Yes, I like the thrill of speed on a motorride. Here, take

this helmet and get on.

And with a roar, we set off. I am clutching the body of the man I love. I'm dreaming and maybe I'm fantasizing about certain things. I'm carefree city girl who believes in Prince Charming. He kidnaps me to offer me the love of a knight on a steed. To have me all to himself. Oh, it's so deliciously romantic!

I don't really know where he's taking me, but it matters little because I could go anywhere with him. The streets go past before my eyes. I imagine myself being abducted and taken to an unknown destination.

Finally, we stop in front of a building. The dream fades away.

I ask myself why we are here, I suddenly get anxious.

The elevator takes us to the top floor and bring us directly to an apartment.

- Welcome to my house, Diane.

And he lets me enter first.

I open my eyes wide to see where he lives. It's small, in fact, a studio flat with modern furniture, a sofa of a well-known brand with a coffee table and a few objects here and there.

- Do you sleep on your sofa?
- No, Diane, look at the stairs up there, that's my room. It's a duplex.
- Oh, a duplex, like in the movies!

I'm dazzled, it's the height of chic and modern for me who lives in a very conventional, old-fashioned flat.

- Do you like my bachelor's den, my dwelling?
- Yes, and especially the fashionable neighbourhood, you are lucky enough to live on the Butte Montmartre.
- It's thanks to a friend that I got it, it was a former artist's studio. Come on, let's go up to the room, we can see the sky

through the glass roof and a bit of the Eiffel Tower.

It's true, the top of the tower pierces its nose right into the sky, which on this particular evening is studded with stars. This part of the tower gives me the impression of being a star that the Iron Lady is watching and protecting.

Nicolas takes me into his arms and starts kissing me gently at first then more passionately.

We fall onto the bed. Carefully, he removes my clothes. I don't move, I'm trembling, I say nothing and decide to let fate take its course. This is my first time, I want it to go well and be unforgettable.

I've made up my mind and I want Nicolas to be the one to make me discover love.

- Nicolas, I want to tell you...
- Shh, don't say anything, Diane.

Now we are naked, he caresses me, kisses my body with soft kisses. I am breathless, offered (willing to offer myself) and at the same time frightened at the idea of the act that will follow. This night must be fabulous and indelible. I want it to be etched in my heart and body forever.

We fall asleep after having taking advantage of each other, of the discovery of our bodies.

I open my eyes first later that night. I am in his arms, my private parts still on fire but soothed. I'm not a little girl any more.

Subsequently, his eyes start blinking and he holds me tighter.

- What time is it?
- Three o'clock, baby.

He calls me his baby, I'm ecstatic.

- My God, it's late, I have to go home, my parents will start worrying about me if they don't see me this morning. They might call the police.

- No, stay on, sleep here.
- I can't, Nic. They'll panic if I don't come home, you don't know them.

Actually, I don't know what to call him now that we're... closer and I hastily hit upon the word Nic, not daring to say darling.

- OK baby, if it doesn't bother you to take a cab, I'm exhausted and can't visualise myself giving you a lift on my bike.
- No, sure, just order a taxi for me.

There's a taxi stand just downstairs; I'll walk down with you there.

I go to the bathroom to freshen up and get dressed, still shaking from what has just happened.

A taxi is parked and I jump in.

- Please take the young lady home.

And he slips 50 francs into my hand.

- Yes, sir.

Nicolas kisses me and I feel my body yearning for him, wanting him.

I whisper my desire in his ear.

He kisses my lips tenderly and says nothing.

- Shall we make a move, little lady? the driver says impatiently.

I am sad to leave him. The car is already swerving in and out through the still empty streets.

I now see this Paris that I love in quite a different perspective, with stars in my heart and hearts in my eyes.

The next morning my mother comes to wake me up.

- My darling, get up, you've already had two calls.

My heart starts to pound, was it Nicolas who called?

- Who phoned Mum?
- Gerald, your agent, and Robert, the photographer.
- Ah... I say in a disappointed tone.
- Were you expecting another call?
- Yes! Nicholas.
- Well, get up my dear, I'll make you some breakfast.

I'm another person, my body is still sore and shaking from the night I spent in Nicolas' arms.

Will my mother realise the change that has taken place in me? Will she see that her little girl has become a woman?

No, she doesn't. She serves me my morning snack as usual. Then I phone Gerald.

- Gerald, how are you?
- Fine, Diane. Did you have a good evening with Nicolas?
- How did you know that?
- But Paris is small my dear and the world of fashion and nightlife is merely a web of gossip.
- Oh Gerald, it was great and Nicolas is so...

I close my eyes as I think about it and search for my words.

- So wonderful.
- "We'll talk about it again," says Gerald. Think about your career first and I have some things to tell you about Nicolas. Well, phone Robert because he has to carry out some trials on you to choose the suitable swimming costumes and the departure date for Greece is nearing.

I can tell from his voice that Gerald is irritated and even embarrassed.

- What do you want to tell me about Nicolas, Gerald?
- Nothing special, darling, but watch out for your little

heart.

And he hangs up.

I am suddenly nervous, questioning myself about what he actually meant by that remark. I'll go to the agency tomorrow to see him face to face. I call Robert at once, who is in a hurry and fixes an appointment for me two days later.

I'm brooding about what Gerald has to say and I'm surprised at what's happening to me with Nicolas.

In fact, I'm feel quite well. Things to tell me, things to tell me. Nicolas who doesn't call, Nicolas who doesn't call.

All this is going round in my head and instead of being happy, I start getting unhappy.

The happiness I've just experienced and the discovery of life is turning into anguish. I am unhappy: why?

A sudden flashback comes to mind. I see myself in the bedroom of my teenage years, undecided about my life and sad inside not knowing how to move towards happiness.

I hear myself listening to Mozart and Gregorian chants because it used to calm my uneasy frame of mind.

And I'm still toying with the idea of becoming a hermit in Tibet. Yes, to flee, to get away from the tumult of life. To think of others and not of myself.

Meditate and let oneself go.

No Diane, you have to pull yourself together and move on.

I take a deep breath and throw out these crazy ideas that just came into my head.

I hang around all day with a heavy heart. This time my mother realises that I'm not feeling well.

"What's wrong with you, Diane? You're not your usual self,

your face looks fallen with a shadow of sadness."
"I'm having doubts, Mum, about my life."
"But sweetheart, what's going on with you?"
"I'm in love, Mum."
"With Nicolas? It's him, isn't it?"
"Yes, how do you know?"
"I'm a mother, darling."
And I cry in her arms.

The next day I go to the agency with a heavy heart and slow steps. I am worried about what Gerald will tell me about Nicolas.

When I enter, I go straight to my booker's office.

- Hello Gerald.
- Oh, hi sweetie, why such a tiny little voice?
- Just a little tired.

I don't dare tell him the truth and I can't wait for him to bring up the subject, but…

- Good news, you're leaving next week for Greece, the client is in a hurry to finish his catalogue. Tomorrow, when you see Robert, you'll finalize what he's planning for the shoot.

Taking off for Greece, the shoot… Everything gets mixed up in my head and not a word from Nicolas. A tear rolls down my cheek, I wipe it away discreetly but Gerald has seen it.

- Oh dear, Diane, what's the matter? In a whisper, I blabber:
- Nicolas…

Gerald bounces up from his chair and announces to the team.

- I'm taking Diane for a coffee, I'll be back in half an hour.

He grabs me by the arm and a few minutes later I find myself sitting next to him in the bar just round the corner.

He orders two whiskies without even asking me, then hands me the glass and says in a loud voice:
- Drink it.

I take a sip, which burns my throat and makes me cough, but immediately the warmth that goes down into me brings a light hope.
- Gerald, what do you want to tell me about Nicolas? I'm worried, I haven't heard from him, I think I'm in love.
- Diane, it's really serious what I'm going to tell you, don't take offence, but you're young, you don't know life as yet and the fashion world is ruthlessly cruel. Nicolas is not for you, he's gay.

The world suddenly collapses before me, everything starts spinning. It's not true that Nicolas is gay, Gerald is a liar.
- You're a liar! I shout as I stand up. Nicolas is a man, I hate you. I hate you. No! No!

He grabs my arm strongly and makes me sit down again.
- Diane, listen, maybe he loves you but I've never seen him with a woman and you know our world, we gossip, we know who sleeps with whom. Everything is in the open and Nicolas is known as a model. I don't know what happened between you, but be careful. Nicolas is not for you.

I get up and leave without saying a word, with an expressionless face, my soul in pain, my heart wounded and my body bruised from having offered itself to Nicolas.

From a distance, Gerald yells:
- Don't forget that you're leaving in a week, Diane. I count on you! shouts Gerald, as I walk out through the door of the café.

I don't care, I'd like to get away from it all, away from this life. Why don't I go to Tibet and become a hermit?

As soon as I get home, I lock myself in my room, listen to

Gregorian music, burst into tears and sob uncontrollably.

Nicholas, Nicholas, why?

The following days pass painfully for me, Nicolas doesn't phone me and nor does he answer my calls.

Is it true that he is a homosexual? But he loved me, it wasn't a dream, the blood on the sheets is proof that something did happen.

The wrenching pain in my lower abdomen was real, then that heat that had invaded my whole body and that empty head ready to be swept away into infinity, that feeling of fainting.

Is a homosexual capable of giving a woman that kind of pleasure? I sink into a mournful sadness.

No news and the departure date for Greece arrives.

*

I don't utter a word in the car that takes me and part of the team to Orly airport. The client decided that I would be the only model in Greece.

Each selected country will have one model: Italy, Spain, Morocco and Greece. Robert, the photographer, will be expected to arrive two days later with his assistant.

I'm with the hairdresser, the make-up artist and the fashion team, stylist and assistants. But this doesn't make me rejoice one bit. It's the first time I've been on a plane, I'm leaving France to work and I'm going to discover a new country that I don't know, the birthplace of democracy.

It is true that I didn't much care about the history of ancient Greece and its mythology at school. No, I am not at all looking forward to this trip. Only a harrowing music rings through my head, a music with appalling consequences, accompanied by scathing words that torture me…

- Diane, Nicolas is homosexual, homosexual, homosexual.

This word resounds in me and hits me in the heart like the bullets from the gun I would have liked to have had to shoot myself along with this forbidden love that has barely begun.

Away with it! Put an end to all this! Fortunately, in these moments of deep sadness, the Tibetan hermit comes back to my mind.

I want to disappear and meditate for the rest of my life in a cave in Tibet, far from everything, far from these worldly sufferings.

Meditate to the extent of forgetting my fears, to calm myself, to love others without expecting anything in return… But I am not a Buddhist and I have to face the life that is opening up before me.

I'm currently leading a life where emphasis is put entirely on the physical aspect without focusing on the mind and it is this destiny that has crossed my path.

The path leading to Greece is full of agony and sorrow, where I have to suppress my feelings and give the best of myself without qualms if I want to continue in this field.

We are about to land and I haven't exchanged a single word with the team members during the flight. No one seemed concerned about it, only Christophe, the make-up artist, asked me at the beginning of the trip if air journeys make me panic.

I simply nodded and I think the word got through because everybody left me in peace.

Upon disembarking the plane, a suffocating heat takes over

me, and makes me feel we are indeed in Greece.

Once we have collected our luggage and passed through customs (where I am complimented), we reach our cars that are have been waiting to take us to our hotel in Athens.

I'm drained out, totally lost and disoriented, and I don't even appreciate the scenery outside.

The scorching heat annoys me and makes me drowsy and I hear myself babbling this idiotic sentence:

- But how will Robert be able to photograph in this furnace? The make-up won't hold.

Christophe, who is with me, get annoyed and answers back:

- But my dear, we photograph at dawn and in the evening. During the day, we stay at the hotel pool and as for you, you'll have to stay in the shade. You mustn't get any marks on your skin.

- Oh! I answer.

There is a heavy silence. He must be thinking how dumb and silly I am. Fortunately, we soon reach the five-star hotel where we have been booked, the Divani Caravel Hotel, that is located in the heart of the capital.

I have never stayed in such a place, a palace in a residential area. The first of many to come!

I must admit that staying in luxury hotels is a privilege that I have always enjoyed, of course provided that you can afford it.

I assume I might be required to share my room with one of the girls in the team but no, I'm alone in this beautiful place. Overlooking the pool, huge bathroom, king size bed, balcony.

Everything seems excessively exaggerated to me. I'm far, far away from my teenager's bedroom in Paris!

I make myself at home and sooner than expected, I make an indescribable mess of the place. The suitcases that have just arrived become jewel boxes that I open to unpack my treasures. It keeps me busy for a while and prevents me from thinking too much about my misfortunes.

I am like a princess in her palace. I turn on the television to put on some background music.

I'm lying on the bed sipping some soda that I pulled out of the minibar when the phone starts ringing.

- Diane, it's Christophe. We've decided to go to dinner in the old part of Athens tonight and then go out. Will you care to join us?

- I don't know, I'm a bit tired.

- But my dear, you can't stay alone and brood! Besides, your agency told us to look after you, so make an effort and come with us.

I gasp and say in a tiny voice:

- OK, but not before eight p.m.

- Of course, Diane, there's plenty of time, so don't be late and I'll see you in the hotel lobby.

I hang up. This phone call gives me the idea of calling France.

Want to hear Nicolas' voice and know the truth but I hesitate, I'm afraid, I'm afraid of the real story.

No, it's up to him to contact me, to tell me, to tell me, to tell me... and I burst into tears on the bed. I sob as I scream out Nicolas' name with my head buried in the pillow.

The tears start flowing down my cheeks and I need my mum. Yes, I am still a little girl who wants to be comforted, who is only at the beginning of her adult life.

My job as a model automatically gives me the status of a grown-up person. I am earning money, I am travelling, I've been put on a pedestal in a certain way by projecting my physical image, but I know nothing about life. I know nothing at all.

I calm down and pick up the phone to call my parents. The ringing tone seems to whine into infinity.

Oh no! There's nobody home... when I hear somebody picking it up.

- Hello?
- Mum, it's Diane.
- Oh, my darling! How are you? Did you get here all right? We miss you here.
- Yes, Mum, everything is wonderful but it's so hot and I miss you too. It's lonely being away from you.
- Be careful then, Diane. And in a breath... Nicolas called.

I think I'm fainting when I hear this. Nicholas phoned, so all that wasn't true, he actually phoned!

- Diane, can you hear me?
- Yes, Mum, I can hear you and what did he say?

There was a silence at the end of the line and then:

- Diane, he says he loves you but he can't, it's not possible, he asks you to forgive him and forget him.

I start to cry like a sad child deprived of something. I would have liked to be in my mother's arms, to be rocked and comforted by her, but we are miles apart.

- "My baby," she says, "I love you."
- I love you too, Mum, I'll call you later, I have to go out with the crew.
- My darling, remember that you have your whole life ahead of you and that it's a beautiful one.
- Yes, a big hug and kisses.

I hang up without disclosing any of my feelings and once again I start howling into the pillow:

- NOOOOOOOOOOOOO.

I don't know how long I have been lying there, shaken with sobs.

A ringing sound is heard, way before I have time to react:

- Diane what are you doing? We're in the hall, waiting for you.
- Oh, Christopher, I fell asleep, I'll be down in fifteen minutes.

I rush to the bathroom, take a quick shower, brush my hair and hurriedly dab some cold cream on my face.

I put on the first dress I can get my hands on, dab myself all over with Molinard Habanita perfume and rush downstairs to meet the rest of the crew.

- Diane, you look radiant.

Inside me I am thinking:

By no means from the inside…

But my blossoming youth is glowing in all its splendour and the sadness on my face is totally concealed.

- Thank you, Christophe. So where are we going?
- First to Plaka, which is a typical neighbourhood at the bottom of the Acropolis with taverns where you get Greek specialties. The /concierge gave me a good address.

So let's go there and then we'll see.

- And where are the others?
- We're just the two of us going to dinner, but maybe they'll join us afterwards.

I don't believe a word of it. Gerald must have instructed him to keep an eye on me, to chaperone me and see that I don't fall into the trap of love with the wrong person again.

Outside, although it is evening, the heat is still stifling. We hail a taxi in front of the hotel which stops dead in front of us.

Christophe gives him the address of the restaurant.
- *Ochi*, says the driver, nodding his head up and down.
We take this nod as a confirmation and get into the taxi.
The irritated driver yells at us:
- *Ochi! Ochi!*
But we don't understand, he makes us get out by saying.
- *Ochi, no no.*
That's how we learn our first word of Greek and later the meaning of the head movement. In fact, it's the opposite of French.

"No" means nodding your head up and down and "yes" means turning your head from left to right, which is where the confusion with the taxi driver comes from.

Finally, the hotel concierge orders a car for us and explains where to take us. We speed off and discover Athens by night, the mythical city.

I am not very talkative and Christophe makes conversation by talking about everything and nothing.

The taxi drops us off at the bottom of a flight of stairs and shows us the way to the restaurant.

It is very typical, and the climb takes us to the top of the Parthenon hill. On either side of the old neoclassical buildings, white with Mediterranean blue shutters, plants adorn the balconies.

On the ground floor of the houses, there are souvenir shops glorifying Greece and in the distance the Acropolis, like a goddess contemplating and protecting her city.

Unfortunately, I can't appreciate these landscapes that are so new and unfamiliar to me. They simply remind me of my history classes on ancient Greece, which had never interested me and that had found extremely boring.

After having climbed up I don't know how many steps, we arrive at the "Athena" tavern. It's a beautiful place decorated in Greek style with blue tones where a band is playing typical and lively music.

The owner, a typical dark-haired, Mediterranean looking man with a moustache, welcomes us:

- Welcome to the district of the gods of the Acropolis!

Then comes the waiter, and while giving us the menu, suggests we try an aperitif called "ouzo".

It looks a bit like pastis, maybe a bit stronger. Its aniseed flavour appeals to me and I drink it almost in one gulp.

My head starts spinning immediately, but I enjoy this intoxication that makes me forget my tiredness, my negative emotions and Nicolas.

All of a sudden, I become talkative and start chatting away, and just as Christophe was doing in the taxi on our way here, I start talking about everything and nothing.

I talk about how happy I am to be a model, how lucky I am in general, about being here in Greece and doing photos for a famous swimming costume catalogue.

Christophe, on the other hand, tells me about his life, his childhood in Nice, his divorced parents, the discovery of his homosexuality as a teenager, how lucky he was to have come later to Paris and to be able to live his life freely.

He is older than me but not much older. He is legally an adult, but we recognise that we are still very young and that life is still a puzzle for us.

I then bring up the subject about Nicolas because I want to know what he thinks of him.

I sob as I finish my story. Christophe did not interrupt me and listened attentively, just nodding his head to encourage me to continue.

He takes me by my hand, kisses it and says gently:

- My beautiful, Diane, don't cry. We are in an environment where everyone sleeps with everyone else and it is true that the boys are often homosexual. Your Nicolas undoubtedly has feelings for you, but if he prefers men, it's difficult for him to have a real relationship with you, and he will never be able to fulfill your desires as a woman. I know it was a bad experience for you, but you have your whole life ahead of you to find your prince charming and your true love. Make him a friend. I'm sure you'll be able to count on him and he'll support you and listen to you in your moments of sadness.

My tears have dried and I take Christophe's hand, give him a friendly kiss and say:

- Thank you.
- What if we went out dancing? Let's enjoy life, my beautiful Diane.
- You're right, let's live it up and enjoy life!

We are all excited, like children. We ask the waiter if he knows a trendy club. He tells us about the Acropolis, which is apparently the most fashionable place *par excellence* for Athenian nights.

Before leaving, the restaurant owner offers us a last drink and we leave the place already quite high.

The disco is not far away, we walk to it singing songs and laughing like crazy.

The Acropolis is in the centre of Athens, near Syntagma

Square, and is located in the basement of a building.

When we arrive, it is already packed, with people dancing on the dance floor which is on a raised platform.

We sit down at the bar and straight away order two whiskies.

- Let's dance, Diane.

We've totally gone wild, the mixture of all those alcohols is having its effect. I swirl, giggle, feel light and relieved at last. I feel good. My head is no longer thinking and brooding.

After half an hour of fun, we return to the bar. Christophe is a charming pal and I enjoy his company. We talk endlessly, as if we've known each other forever.

A group of men in their twenties arrive and take a seat at the bar next to us. They talk loudly, laugh and seem to be having a good time too. After ten minutes they talk to us, ask us where we are from and what we are doing here in Greece.

Christophe, an incorrigible chatterbox, gives a detailed account of why we are here. As a result, they all get interested in me, asking me my first name and inviting me to dance.

As they are very nice, I accept. We all have fun together as if we were old friends.

We are now at the bar laughing when a man approaches the group.

My eyes meet his and for a moment we stare at each other intensely. I don't understand what's happening to me, I'm hypnotised by this man. I am overwhelmed, electrified.

He's the one, I think.

I don't know how or why this idea comes to my mind.

Christophe sees my discomfort and asks me what's going on.

- I think I've drunk too much, let's go home.

As we leave, I see the man in deep conversation with our new friends. We say goodbye and as we are leaving the room our eyes meet again.

I'm all flustered by him again. It's incomprehensible what's happening to me. It is unreal.

In the taxi, I close my eyes, the window is open and the wind, still warm at that hour, slashes on my face. Only he is hovering in my mind.

The next day, when I wake up, I have a hangover and his image still haunts me. Who is this stranger? I don't know his name, nor if I will ever see him again one day.

Diane, you're crazy, I say to myself. *Yesterday you were thinking only of Nicolas and today of someone else. You're out of your mind.*

I have the whole day to myself. Christophe left me a message saying that Robert and his assistant were late, that they would be arriving later, at least not in two days as planned.

The photo shoot will start a day after their arrival. So that gives me some time to myself.

I decide to discover the city on my own, to explore the Plaka district and to visit the Acropolis. I feel like walking, and want to get lost in the city.

A compelling urge to phone Nicolas again overcomes me, but this time I'm no longer the pleading little girl throwing myself at his feet. I just want to know the facts. I go ahead and call him.

I'm about to hang up when suddenly a sleepy voice picks up the phone.

- Hello?
- It's Diane.

There is total silence at the other end. I take a deep breath and at one go I say:

- I'm in Greece, Nicolas, and I perfectly understand your confused state of mind, so let's not talk about it any more and let's just remain friends. You are important to me, you have made me a woman, even if it is difficult to accept that your love for me is impossible. I would like to hear from you whether all that I have been hearing about you is indeed the truth.
- Forgive me, Diane, for the pain I did to you, but of course I want to be your friend because I love you very much, I would have loved to fulfill my duty and offer you a peaceful life of eternal bliss, but I can't go any further, I'm sorry for the pain I have caused you. And in spite of everything that people have said about me, know that you are the woman of my life and that you will be the one and only.
- Thank you, Nicolas, you too are very important to me.
- Call me when you return from Greece, Diane.

We don't wish to pursue the conversation any further.

We hang up, I am still thinking. A first love and an unfeasible love. What a good way to take the first step. Is this life?

But the image of the man I saw the day before keeps coming back to me. I've just spoken to the man whom I was still pining for in my mind a few days before and here I am now, already thinking of another one. I don't understand. Is this really love?

I'm outside, walking through the streets at random, hoping not to get lost and find my way to Plaka. The heavy heat that falls over the city does not bother me today, it penetrates into me and gently enervates me, making me slowly drowsy.

I feel like a robot walking mechanically on the burning concrete, free of all thoughts, with an empty mind, but despite everything, I feel good. My footsteps lead me to a large square, Omonia.

I am thirsty but I want to get to Plaka first, I don't know why I want to reach this area quickly.

I ask for directions because I've lost my way, now I don't know where I am any more. Finally, I'm told that I am only five minutes away from my destination.

In a short time, I find myself in Monastiraki.

I walk up the street in front of me, wide-eyed at all the souvenir shops.

There is an abundant array of handicrafts representing Greek gods as well as replicas of ancient jewellery displayed everywhere. It's beautiful and I take pleasure in reading the names of the gods and goddesses that come to mind. I find out that Diane is Artemis in Greek and the twin of Apollo. I like being the sister of a god.

A beautiful shady square appears on the horizon, at the end of a shopping street.

I sit down at a table under a parasol to protect myself from the sun and order a soda to quench my thirst.

I still remember the name of the street, *Odos Panos*.

I have walked a lot and I am exhausted. The drink flows delicately down my throat and I let the ice cubes melt gently in my mouth to enjoy the freshness it gives me.

I think about the last few days, about my life, about Nicolas, and finally, I realise what a privileged person I am. I close my eyes and my classmates come to mind. I visualise them sitting in the classroom.

A smile comes to my lips.

How lucky I am, at my age, to already know everything that I am experiencing! I am really relishing this moment of happiness.

A shadow is cast over my face, I open my eyes, a waiter is standing in front of me smiling.

He explains in broken English that some young people want to buy me a drink and points at them.

I didn't notice them when I arrived, I just wanted to quench my thirst, but now that I look at them, their faces look familiar.

Oh my goodness! It's true, no it isnt't! They are the same friends from the disco, I can't believe my eyes.

And who is with them? He!

Yes, it's him all right, he's turning his back and seems to be engaged in conversation with one of the group members. They start waving frantically at me and shout at me to come and join them. He does not react to my presence. How small the world is... or a stroke of good luck is just round the corner!

My upbringing forbids me to sit with men at their table. It's not considered proper for an unaccompanied woman to join a group of men, but I'm just dying to go to them.

I ask the waiter in my broken Greek:

- *Ena frappè parakalo.*

That's what I've heard before and I merely repeat it.

The waiter is amused and gives me a friendly smile.

A few minutes later he brings me my frappé, which is actually an iced coffee.

I don't go to the young people's table but raise a toast with my glass by saying "cheers" from a distance.

They look disappointed but smile at me. They again make gestures to me to join them.

I shake my head as if to say no and smile too. I am amused by this little game, but I wish the stranger would turn around and look at me, but no, he ignores me.

One of the young men leaves the group and hesitantly walks towards me shyly.

He asks me if he can sit at my table. I obviously agree because they are all very friendly.

He speaks English better than I do. He introduces himself very officially, which is very funny.

- My name is Yorgos Papadros and I am with my friends. We are students here in Athens, except Yannis, who lives in London.

And he points out to the stranger. Now I know his name and I know where he lives.

I explain to him that I am a model and that we are going to do some photos in the next few days for a fashion catalogue.

He looks at me dumbfounded, his mouth wide open.

- So it's true what Christophe told us? Are you a model? That's why you're so beautiful and so tall. You look like a goddess!

Giggling, I tell him:

- I am a goddess, my name is Diane, Artemis in Greek.

And we laugh heartily at the top of our lungs. His friends look at us in surprise and must be wondering why we are laughing so loudly.

Come to our table, goddess Diane.

- No I can't, I have to leave now.
- Then let's meet tonight at the Acropolis.
- Maybe we will.

I grab hold of my bag and get up, thanking him for his kindness. I still look as if I'm trying to away from there.
- See you tonight, beautiful goddess.
- *Yassou Yorgos.*

I love to practice the few words of Greek I have retained.

I wave goodbye to the group, all of them greeting me except the stranger who doesn't even deign to turn around.

What on earth does he think of himself?

*

I jauntily reach the hotel all perky and cheerful and phone Christophe from the reception.

Nobody answers. I decide to go by the swimming pool to see whether I can find him and indeed, I see him on his deckchair, a glass in his hand.
- Diane, where have you been? I've been looking for you and getting worried. Just inform me in advance before you go out.

I forgot that he has to act as a chaperone.
- I'm so sorry Christophe, I felt like going out and being alone for a while.
- I understand my dear, but warn me next time. So what did you do?
- Oh, I took a walk at the Plaka, I looked at the shops, but you'll never guess what happened to me.
- Oh my God, you worry me! Nothing serious I hope.
- No no, I met some people you know too.
- Oh, really? French people?
- No, Greeks.
- But I don't know any Greeks.

- Last night, at the disco, the ones at the bar... Well, they were at a café terrace where I was.
- And then?
- Well, then they offered me a drink and one of them whose name was Yorgos came to my table and we talked.
- And they are nice?
- Yes, lovely people, they asked me to meet them tonight at the Acropolis, I said maybe. Tell me, would you like to come with me tonight? I want to go out.

I hide the fact from Christophe that, in the group, the Unknown Stranger was there and that my greatest desire in the world is to see him.

- Yes, why not, I certainly don't want to remain here in the room. But let's have dinner at the hotel, it will be easier. We can then get ready afterwards at leisure to go out.
- You're so sweet, Christophe, I love you.
- I know, he says, laughing. So let's meet at eight o'clock in the restaurant.

I go up to my room, I'm floating on cloud nine. I'm going to see him again. See the Unknown Stranger again.

As soon as I get ready, I call Christophe.
- I am ready, Christophe, I tell him in English (normally we speak French).
- OK, darling, in fifteen minutes at the reception.
- Christophe is all smiles when he sees me.
- Diane, I made friends with the waiter at the swimming pool and he told me about a tavern near the hotel which I heard serves typical Greek food, so I'll take you there, beauty.
- Why not Christophe.

The dinner is delicious. I discover authentic Greek cuisine, sun-dried octopus, salad with feta cheese, tzatziki, this yoghurt with cucumber, and a sweet dish made of angel hair vermicelli, honey and nuts which is so deliciously tempting, a real treat but very sweet, so to be eaten in moderation for me. Not to mention just a few along with an array of other good things.

Everything is perfect and the two hours spent in Christophe's company seem like only a few minutes. He is really an admirable chaperone and takes his role seriously.

He has no idea that I have guessed that he has been instructed to keep an eye on me.

We arrive at the Acropolis around eleven thirty p.m. The disco is packed; there are no free tables or places at the bar. It's too dark to see if our friends are there.

- Good evening, would you like to join us? It is the Unknown Stranger who is addressing us.

My entire body starts trembling.

- I am Yorgos' friend, we are sitting at the back, if you want to come to our table, you are welcome.

I look at Christophe, thinking he's going to answer, but God knows where he has suddenly gone off; maybe he's noticed a good-looking boy.

I give him a discreet nudge.

- Sure, we're following you.

We are now sitting at a table with Yorgos, the unknown Yannis and two other friends of theirs.

I'm feeling rather awkward and don't say much, but Christophe is at ease and talks about our life and what we are doing in Athens.

- So it's true, the goddess is a model?
- The goddess? asks Christopher, puzzled.
- Yes, Diane, Artemis in Greek, the twin sister of Apollo, Yorgos replies seriously.
- Oh right... but yes, Diane is a goddess, a future star, says Christophe in a pedantic tone.

Everyone starts clapping and praising me, and I feel terribly uncomfortable.

Yannis sees my embarrassment and suddenly gets up.
- Diane, let's go and dance.

And he takes me by the arm without even waiting for my answer.

I find myself on the dance floor with the Unknown Stranger. I don't know how to behave with him. His presence is so disturbing and I'm totally confused.

Everything about him attracts me: his looks, his eyes, his voice. Deep down in my mind I hear a voice:
- This is Him.

And what about Him?

The modern music gives way to traditional Greek music and we return to the table.
- Goddess, now you will hear the music of our country, it will produce vibrations within you, Yorgos tells me.

Musicians have taken their places and are playing Greek tunes. Some men stand up and dance to the rhythms of the bouzouki.

Yannis asks me if I like it.
- Yes, it's new to me, but isn't it the music of the gods? In that case I like it, I say, laughing.

My mind and ears are captivated by the song that is now playing. I don't understand it, but the tune and the words speak

out to me. I like this song that goes deep into my being.
- Yannis, I like it very much. What is it called?
- *Ya panta mazi,* he says. Which means: forever together.
- Forever together, *Ya panta mazi.*

I hum this tune that fills me with joy and love without knowing why.
- I also love this song, Diane.

He is the only one who doesn't call me Goddess.

Our eyes dive into the abyss of our gaze and say incredible things to each other.

Our lips are just about to come closer together but our friends unintentionally interrupt our blossoming romance, without actually noticing anything.
- Let's all go and dance the sirtaki!

Yannis takes me by the hand.
- *Ya panta mazi*, he whispers in my ear.

The evening is absolutely magical from all aspects. The hours go by without my realizing how much time has passed. We all have fun together, but in fact I am alone with Yannis.

My new friends do not exist, even if I talk to them or dance with them. Only Yannis counts.

My mind and my body already belong to him.

What else does life have in store for me? I have hardly come to terms with what happened with Nicolas, and here I am, falling in love once again!

I know nothing about men and I'm so young... What have I got myself into now?

*

Christophe and I walk back to the hotel, and are obviously totally drunk. Nobody noticed that I quietly gave my address to Yannis so that he could join me later. I don't want anyone to know that we're going to see each other.

This night is a true discovery for me, my body vibrates wonderfully, harmoniously in Yannis' arms. We love each other until the early break of dawn in an unsuspected and burning fusion of bodies.

Nicolas has made me a woman, but Yannis, with his virile strength, his passion and his love, has transported me to sheer ecstasy towards the stars of cloud nine.

I am a woman in love and I know what that really means, when the mind and body are united as one.

But how am I going to handle this situation? Robert and the rest of the crew will be arriving soon and we are going to start working. I have no more desire to work, I just want to stay with Yannis.

I don't know anything about him, but I'm ready to follow him to the end of the world.

We escape in the course of the morning after having slept little, yes, very little indeed. He takes me to a tavern by the sea where we nourish ourselves with delicious food and with each other's looks. We are slowly getting to discover each other.

He tells me that he is on holiday with his parents and that he lives in London. Cautiously, he confesses that he is married to an Englishwoman, that he has a son who is with him in Athens.

My world collapses. Once again, it is not easy and the desire of my monastery life in Tibet comes to mind. Is it an escape or a protection? I don't know.

He perceives my dismay in my silence, my torment and pain,

and tries to comfort me.

- Diane, I am separated from her and we are getting divorced.

Tears roll down my cheeks.

- Don't cry little girl, I love you.

I hardly know him and already my whole being loves him. He is my destiny. I have come all the way to Greece to meet him and live this passion. I am absolutely sure. But how will it work out, with him in London, me in Paris and that too travelling frequently for my work? Is it true that he's in the process of divorcing? Maybe it's just a trick to get me.

Seeing my confusion, he adds:

- Little girl, let's continue to live and see what the future has in store for us.

I am distraught and do not know what to say.

«Yes» is the only word that comes out.

- Let's go for a walk by the sea, he suggests.

The sea is a deep blue with turquoise reflections.

- Your eyes are the colour of water, little girl, you are like the sea, calm and at times turbulent. I can read you, Diane.

We look at each other so intensely that I am disturbed. I feel as if he really is reading me and that I already belong to him completely.

I thrust myself into him and we become one. I immerse myself in his honey coloured eyes and drown blindly in them.

I am deeply in love with him, but I am trapped in a life I can no longer control.

- But how are we going to start a relationship, Yannis? I'll be busy with my work, then I'll go back home to Paris.

- Hush, don't think about anything, live in the moment,

have faith.

And he kisses me so passionately that I swoon into unsuspected depths.

Unfortunately, evening arrives and it's time for me to go back to the hotel. I could stay in his arms forever.

He drops me off in a taxi and plans to come to meet me later.

The hotel concierge calls out to me:
- Miss, you have some messages.

I take them and see that they are all from Christophe.

Thirty minutes later, there's a knock on my door.

Surely it must be Christophe who is looking for me in a panic, to tell me that Robert is expected to arrive the following day and that we will start the photos the day after tomorrow.

Panic takes hold of me. How will I be able to manage my relationship with Yannis? I have to immediately mention it to Christophe to know more about this.

That's just it, it must be him.

I open the door and Yannis appears, all smiles.
- I couldn't wait, I want you.

He's standing in front of me, impatient. Our bodies are yearning for each other and the fever of desire is mounting within us.

I am naked and love-sick on my bed, conquered.

He has just left when I realise that I know nothing about him, only his first name, but I have neither a phone number to reach him, nor an address, nothing at all.

And he didn't say anything to me, not a word, I don't know

if we'll ever meet again later in life. And I, infatuated and carried away by my desires, didn't ask either.

Maybe I'll never see him again, maybe I was just a toy for him.

I am trapped.

Distraught and desperate, I call Christophe.

- But where have you been Diane?

And I tell him everything.

Christophe listens to me without interrupting and then blurts out:

- Diane, you've got yourself into a real mess, a long-distance romance is always difficult and almost impossible. Besides, with your job, I don't see how you're going to manage.
- Oh don't tell me that, I don't even know how to find him.
- Forget about him for now, darling, because we're starting work, so no sleepless nights, no black circles under the eyes, a glowing, flawless complexion, you have to be available. If Robert notices anything he'll go into a rage and then you won't recognise him. So let's see and I'm here for you, my young damsel in love that you are!

I spend an eventful night, made up of dreams and nightmares during which I see Yannis moving away and becoming smaller and smaller until he disappears.

I wake up with a start, caught up in the torment of this nightmare and at the same time the phone rings like a stab in my heart.

- Hello, I say in a voice hoarse with tears.
- Diane, it's Robert.
- Oh Robert, you've arrived!

- Diane, there's a problem with the collection, they're adding pieces that won't be ready for a week, so the crew is packing up and going back to France.

I stammer:

- Going back to France?

In my head, everything is spinning, it's the end of my story, I'll never see him again, once again, I'm devastated.

- But Diane, if you want to stay on here and wait for us you can do so. I've spoken to your agent and maybe it's better that you get some rest before we arrive, because after that we'll work without a break and we'll have to get up early for the light and above all catch up the delay.

A glimmer of hope filters through and I hear myself saying:

- Oh right, I think that's better.

Robert hasn't the faintest idea about what I have in mind and I artfully manage to conceal my joy.

After this phone call it's Christophe who calls me:

- Diane, you know we're going back to Paris.
- Yes, I've just spoken to Robert, but I'm staying on, I have to be hail and hearty when he comes back, he told me.
- On your own? You lucky girl! And what are you going to do during this week?
- Look for him, of course.

The crew leaves the next day and for the first time in my life I am alone, free in this city and scared at the same time but with one goal: to look for him.

I phone my mother to keep her informed on the change of plan.

- But they left you alone? They are crazy!

And she starts her usual lecture of precautions and

recommendations: don't do this, don't go there, go to bed early...

To reassure her, I tell her that I'm being chaperoned by the Greek representative of our modeling agency here in Athens, which is not true; I've simply been given their telephone number in case of emergency.

I can make out that she is reassured, but she still asks me to call her every day.

My only concern right now is to find him. That's all I can think about.

I only know his first name and his friends. No address, no phone number. In fact, I have very little information about him.

*

I feel so helpless and don't know what to do. I decide to go to the swimming pool to change my thoughts and to refresh them.

The pool is deserted, I sit down on a deckchair which I choose in the shade because I must not have any marks on my body.

I close my eyes and dive not into the water but into a gentle lethargy.

The warm sun caresses me and surrounds me with its arms in a benevolent protection. I remember the last few days, Greece and Athens, my meeting with those young people in the square, Yannis, the disco.

The disco, of course. I open my eyes, a smile on my lips.

The disco, maybe that's where I'll see him again. I'm pleased with myself, I think I've found the solution, at least a lead.

In an instant, the day seems to pass quickly and in the

evening I get ready like Cinderella going to the ball in search of her Prince Charming.

I put on a little make-up and then go through my outfits.

I didn't bring too many clothes because I'm here to work and not to go out.

But fate decided otherwise. I decide to wear a blue and white silk backless outfit that dances on my diaphanous skin.

I examine myself in front of the mirror and find myself desirable.

I wait until eleven thirty p.m. to go out. There's no point in going out too early.

I confidently walk into the discotheque but my heart is beating fast inside.

I look straight ahead without glancing left and right. I walk straight to the bar and slide across to the only free stool available. I order a whiskey with Coke and put on a casual attitude whereas everything inside me is boiling.

I shyly look around the room with a carefree indifference. There are already a lot of people and the clouds of thick smoke prevent me from seeing clearly. There are no figures that remind me of Yannis.

I order another drink. I'm starting to get tipsy, my head is spinning, I have to move.

I decide to go dancing despite the lack of desire to jiggle around. As soon as I get to the dance floor and hardly have I started to dance, a pair of arms embraces me from behind.

I think I'll faint, it's him, I've found him! When I hear in my ear:

- Goddess, what a pleasure to have you here!

My world collapses, it's not him but Yorgos.

I turn around and say with an exuberant and silly laugh:
- Yorgos!

Nothing else comes out of my mouth but Yorgos, which I repeat several times, still laughing stupidly.

He invites me to his table, which he is sharing with two friends of his who speak only Greek. He gives them a detailed account of our meeting. They are nice and try to communicate with me, but I'm not really in a mood make light talk.

So I laugh at everything and nothing, in fact I am not really listening to what they are telling me. I pretend to participate, but at some point I manage to slip in:
- What about your other friends, aren't they with you tonight?
- No goddess, we don't see each other all the time.
- Anyway, they are very nice.

*

He has a smile on his lips that I don't know how to interpret. Does he know about me and Yannis? In any case, he doesn't show anything.

I've drunk too much and my friend is becoming a bit too insistent.
- I'm going to go home now, it's time for bed.
- Goddess, come with us to Glyfada to listen to the bouzouki music, he says, hugging me.

I firmly wriggle myself out of his embrace.
- I am tired and need look fresh for the photo shoot. I'm going to take a taxi but I'll be back tomorrow night.

I kiss him on the cheek, wave to his friends and leave.

The warm air outside feels good, I stand outside the entrance for a few seconds. The harsh light of a street lamp dazzles my eyes, making me blink. I can't see clearly when I think I can see him.

Is it my imagination or a drunken hallucination? Oh no, it's not! It is him. I shudder and cannot move.

He arrives with a group of friends. I think I'm going to faint when I realise that it's indeed him in flesh and blood. Has he seen me?

They are noisy, talking in Greek, very loudly. I assume they are drunk.

They are all moving towards me and suddenly, as they get closer, he sees me.

His eyes glare at me, he talks to them, comes towards me and seizes me with force by the arm.

- What are you doing here, little girl, are you all alone?

I stammer:

- Yes.
- Let's go.

He says something in Greek to his friends, hails a taxi and pushes me in.

Then I understand that he is giving the address of my hotel.

- You've been drinking, little girl, that's not good. And what are you doing alone at night in Athens? Where are your friends? Aren't you supposed to be working?
- Yes, but it's postponed until next week, so everyone's gone except me.
- Why didn't you go too?
- For your sake, to see you, to see you again. You left like a thief. It was impossible for me to go back to France.

He takes me in his arms and kisses me tenderly, whispering in my ear:

- Little girl, little girl, you are mine…

*

The night is short and it sweeps me into an unexpected whirlwind of ecstasy.

His skin electrifies me, his kisses bewitch me, his body calls me at every moment.

I could live simply survive on his love forever.

I am madly in love. Fate has sent me to Athens to experience the happiness of being in harmony with a man. I fall asleep in his arms, nourished by love and fulfillment.

I spend the night rocked by his breath blowing on me, the embrace of his arms is like chains of love that protect me and in which I cuddle myself. I belong to him.

The next day, after breakfast, he asks me to get ready and we go to the beach.

On the way out, he tells me that we'll drop by his parents' house to pick up his son who is on holiday with him.

I am surprised that he wants to introduce me to him. I don't remember him telling me about his son, but it's true that we didn't talk much during our lovemaking. Or maybe I didn't want to hear it.

He makes me wait in the taxi at the bottom of an insignificant building where his parents live. I am nervous about seeing his son. I know now that his name is Daniel and that he is four years old. How should I behave? Just being natural is the best.

The initial contact is difficult, he refuses to say hello and completely ignores me. He only wants his father's arms.

Yannis talks to him about me, tells him I'm his friend, but

that doesn't change anything.

We are in the suburbs of Athens, in Glyfada, by the sea, sitting on the deck chairs of a private beach, under a parasol like the ideal couple: Dad, Mum and baby. I don't mind, I admit, and I start dreaming of having a child with Yannis.

Daniel and I don't really get along very well. Does he understand anything about the relationship between his father and me? Yannis does not hide his feelings and is as attentive to me as to his son.

I remember an incident that clearly shows the child's hostility towards me.

Yannis went to get a drink and while he was doing so, I was in charge of keeping an eye on Daniel.

Of course, the brat escapes and I start running after him. People say to me:

- Your son is over there.

But he runs away quickly. Finally, I manage to catch hold of him and the little monster starts struggling and pulls my hair hard, and that was my first encounter with Daniel.

The next few days we go back to the beach but without him, and I think Yannis realised that it was better to avoid conflicts.

We spend every night together, and at the slightest touch, we start desiring each other, it's absolutely magnetic.

Our hands are always searching for each other and so are our mouths. The time spent with him is an ecstasy, I feel light, happy and loved.

We make plans and Yannis is already talking about a baby, a little girl who would look like me, and as for myself, I start making plans about getting married.

That is the delicate point and he tells me that I have to wait, that as soon as he is divorced, we will get married in Athens in the Orthodox Church. I believe him.

The days pass in loving each other but also in bickering. I am jealous and afraid of losing him, I madly in love. He represents everything I want in a man: caring, sensual, humorous... And there is an undeniable chemistry between us.

The fateful day when I have to start work is fast approaching, and Robert's phone reminds me of my duties. They are all arriving in two days and I have to be ready for them.
I tell Yannis, who looks pensive.
- Diane, Daniel's mother, phoned my parents and I have to take him back to London.
I'm stunned.
- But we won't see each other again, it's not possible!
And I start crying.
- Don't cry little girl, I'll be back soon.
- And when are you leaving?
- Tomorrow night.
And all the misfortunes of the world come crashing down on me. They are no longer tears but the Niagara Falls.
- Little girl, you'll be able to concentrate on your work without my getting in your way all the time.
- But I won't be able to live without you.
It is our bodies that answer my questions, he makes love to me like a god.
He is my Greek god and I am his goddess in his arms.
He promises to call me at the hotel as soon as he reaches England.

We part with a sad good-bye, I feel as if I am losing a part of myself.

When will I ever see him again?

I am alone now in my room. I am crying, I am drained of my tears. I am still recollecting our embraces in my mind. I am really a lost little girl lost and madly in love.

There are several knocks on the door, each one louder and louder, but I don't react. This time it starts banging and I hear the noise, I get up and open the door.

Robert is standing in front of me with unfamiliar expression that I have never seen before, closed and astonished.

- Diane, what's wrong with you? Have you seen your face?

He pushes me and comes in, dragging me inside:

- Look at you, you're pale, your skin is all shriveled.

Robert, I've been ill, I've been throwing up all night, I say, not knowing what to reply to give.

- Lie down, I'll call a doctor.

The doctor diagnoses indigestion and prescribes rest.

Robert is reassured.

- A good night's sleep and everything will be fine and tomorrow we'll start work. So rest, sleep and don't go out, Diane. Christophe and Dodo will come tomorrow at six o' clock to do your hair and make-up. We'll leave for Cape Sounion at around seven o'clock.

There is no more time to go to Mykonos, we'll remain on the coast near Athens.

The next morning, very early, I meet Christophe, the make-up artist, accompanied by the hairdresser Dodo. I took complete rest and they find me looking radiant and bright.

Christophe takes me aside and asks for an update on the latest developments.

- He's gone, I say sadly.
- You can't trust men, it's terrible, he moans.

All that I now want is to stay at the hotel to wait for his phone call. But I'm a professional and don't want to disappoint anyone.

I am now fully made up, ready and obedient.

We are on a deserted beach and start the photos. The swimming costumes are beautiful and I am happy to pose.

Robert is happy with the light, with me and we are making good progress with our programme.

Every day at noon, when we return to the hotel, I rush to see if I have any messages, but the answer is always the same: no.

The week goes by waiting for his call. I'm unhappy but I manage to hide my feelings because I mustn't disappoint Robert, who is delighted with the photos and with me. It's all in the box, as Robert says, we're done with it!

We have to leave in two days and I don't know where I stand. Once again I've made a mistake. In fact, I'm a fool who gets carried away by the first person who comes along and thinks she knows the meaning of love.

Love makes me stupid and is not for me, I think.

I would be much better off in the Himalayan mountains meditating and not suffering. But I am far from Tibet and I don't know yet what meditation means.

I'm just a lonely, immature little girl who thinks she's an adult, but no matter how much I'm transformed, how desirable I'm made to be to sell a product, that's not me, and Yannis is right when he calls me a "little girl".

I am just a baby in a woman's body. I'm just a physical form but from all points of view that suits me perfectly for the time being because I don't know anything about life and seeing myself in magazines and recognised inflates my importance and feeds my ego.

That's what makes me exist, the gaze of others telling me I'm beautiful. But now it's Yannis' gaze, the one he has on me, that I want and that I miss.

- Yannis! Yannis, where are you? Do call me.

Robert has booked the pool for our last evening with a Lebanese buffet to celebrate the end of the shoot. Everyone is happy, drinking, having fun, but I'm not in the mood to feast.

I'm totally crestfallen at the moment, we're leaving tomorrow at the end of the morning and still no news, so what is to be done?

Christophe joins me and, with his usual kindness, manages to get me moving.

- Diane, forget about him and come and have a drink. Get drunk, it will do you good.

Christophe is crazy, but that's just what I do.

Once back in my room, drunk, I throw myself on my bed and fall asleep immediately.

I dream that the telephone is ringing and ringing away.

I wake up with a start, because it's true, the phone is ringing non-stop.

In a blurred voice, I'm able to blurt out a painful "hello".

- Little girl, it's me. Did I wake you up?

It's Him, Him! He hasn't forgotten me.

- Yannis, is that you? I waited so long for your phone call…

- Sorry, I couldn't make it before, problems with Daniel's mother, but I'll come back to see you.
- Yannis, I'm going back to Paris tomorrow, we've finished.
- I'll come and see you in Paris then.
- Yannis, I must tell you, but not having heard from you, I accepted a contract in Israel for fashion shows.
- But when are you leaving?
- In a week, to give us time to do trials and rehearsals.
- I'm coming to Paris, give me your phone. I'll call you and tell you exactly when I'm arriving. We need to meet, little girl, we need to talk about us. I've missed you.

I'm upset, I shouldn't have accepted this new assignment but I was so desperate that I had to leave and when Gerald offered it to me, I didn't hesitate to accept it.
- OK, Yannis, I'll wait for you. Come quickly.
- I promise, little girl.

*

How wonderful it feels to be back home and to see the family again!
- Mum, I'm so happy to see you again!
- Me too, my dear, you are absolutely glowing. You have to tell me about it.

After putting my things away, we sit in the living room and I give her a detailed account about my stay in Greece, the five-star hotel, the city, the beautiful pictures Robert took and I can't help mentioning Yannis.
- Mum, I went out in the evening and met some Greeks.
- Oh that's nice and are they nice?

- Yes, very nice, especially the one I met, Yannis.
- And what do you mean, darling?
- That I'm in love, he's twenty-six, lives in London, is married and getting a divorce and has a son called Daniel.
- Darling, what kind of a mess have you got yourself into now?
- But it's all right, Mum, he loves me. He's coming to Paris to see me.
- And what does this Yannis do?
- He works in the advertising field in London.
- Oh, I forgot to tell you!
- You make me feel scared.
- No, no, I'm going to Israel to represent French fashion. It's very well paid.
- But you just got back home! And for how long are you going to be away again?
- Only two weeks.
- Diane, I can't keep pace with you any longer, you're in love, you're going to Israel, I've lost control over your life…
- Mum, have faith, life is good for me, I'm doing a job I enjoy, I travel, I'm in love.
- Think about your parents, we are worried about you, your father and me, everything has gone so fast…
- I understand that. But I am happy, isn't that what all parents want for their child?
- Yes. We'll talk about it with your father tonight, if you're there of course.

Dad is absolutely delighted to see me and during dinner I tell him what I've already told my mother. Greece, my plans and Yannis.

- But that's great, darling, it's all good for you!

Dad understands and gives me his consent. I am surprised that he accepts so easily, he who usually has reservations. He is seeing me succeed, that's what matters to him.

I feel I am being understood.

I'm under pressure because I'm expecting Yannis's phone call, which doesn't come and the preparations for my trip to Israel are stressing me out.

Everyday there are rehearsals involving trials and accessories for the show. I've never done this before and it's going to be more of a performance than a fashion show.

We are five girls and two boys. We rehearse at the Wacker studio, which is very well known in Paris among dancers who come for dance classes or to prepare shows.

A choreographer directs us and gets mad at us because we are not dancers but ordinary models.

She has five days to teach us everything. The theme of the show is the four seasons that are divided into four items.

The Chamber of French Couture organises these fashion shows and wants to showcase French ready-to-wear. They want us to represent France with dignity, so no mistakes.

Every evening, I come home exhausted and happy to see that I'm succeeding, but above all that I'm enjoying it enormously.

Finally, Yannis calls me to tell me that he is coming the next day and asks me to book a hotel.

I inform my parents about his arrival, with a bit of apprehension, and that I'll be sleeping over.

I am surprised at their reaction because they take it

lightheartedly.

In fact, they are more worried about my trip to Israel than about my relationship. They don't comment too much on my future contract, but I know them and their silence speaks volumes.

Things are moving really fast, Yannis coming, rehearsals ending and the departure date approaching. A lot of stress that I have to deal with...

At this point, as usual, I quickly fall back into my beliefs and imagine myself in my life as a hermit in Tibet.

This calms me down because what I am experiencing at the moment is the opposite of a meditation.

I haven't seen Yannis since I left Greece, will the charm still work?

For the sake of convenience, I booked a hotel near the rehearsal studio.

Now he's there. The hotel becomes our home, just like in Athens.

During the day I rehearse and as soon as I get home, we love each other. A love story is really starting to blossom. Nothing has changed since the first day.

I introduce him to my parents at a dinner at home. My parents are taken in by his charm and accept him immediately. My mother whispers in my ears:

- He's a good-looking man, you make a good couple.

They see that I'm in a sincere relationship and give me their approval.

We're very close, we can't stop touching each other. We need tactile moments just as we need air to breathe. We are one heart that loves itself.

Everything is going so fast... It is already time for me to leave. We decide that upon my return, I will go to London to join him. This time I have a phone number.

Did he want to be sure of our feelings before finally giving me his contact details? That's the impression I get.

Israel is a success. The country is beautiful and enchanting, steeped in its ancient history that touches you to the core. Jerusalem overwhelms me. I get goose pimples when I enter the old city.

Invisible energies coming from a bygone era invade me, an unimaginable sensation.

The audience applauds wholeheartedly after our show. The people simply adore us and welcome us as if we were stars.

We perform in Tel Aviv, Haifa and Jerusalem in theatres where the show opens with a very famous Israeli singer, the Johnny Hallyday of Israel, *ST*.

I must admit that I am not indifferent to him, he keeps coming up to me to talk to me and furthermore, even tries to flirt with me, telling me that I am beautiful, glowing with freshness, intelligent, that he has never seen a girl like me. I'm not interested in him at all, but I leave him guessing because I enjoy hearing all these compliments.

I'm a little girl who doesn't realise what she's doing.

Does being on a stage, being applauded, feeling admired, is this turning my head? Maybe it is indeed.

One evening, in Tel Aviv, after our parade, I sneak into the hall to see ST's show. He is undoubtedly excellent and sings well. At one point, he starts talking to his audience and instantly all eyes turn to me.

The girls start screaming but he calms them down. I'm told later that he announced that I was the girl he liked.

Did he just do this to excite his fans or is it true? All I know is that he is married to an American woman. But then, there's no such thing as faithfulness in this business. The temptations are too strong and too easy.

Despite my indifference, he gives me his address and tells me that I am welcome at his place.

We take pictures to remember those beautiful moments and he asks me to promise to come to Tel Aviv to see him.

I say yes, knowing that I will not. I am faithful to Yannis.

Israel is now coming to an end and I will always have wonderful memories of it, but what matters most is that I am going to meet my lover again.

I buy the newspapers in which they are talking about us. The press has been glorifying our fashion shows and I pick up several copies for my press book, the agency and my parents.

I leave with a smile on my face, overwhelmed by what I have just experienced, all of which will remain engraved in my memory.

My return is the beginning of a new era for me.

As soon as I arrive, I phone Yannis who asks me to come as soon as possible because he is missing me.

I inform Gerald, my booker, that I need a holiday, that he should not make any appointments for the next two weeks.

After kissing my parents' goodbye and spending two days with them so they can have me to themselves, I fly to London.

The reunion is enchanting and I finally get to know Yannis'

London life. I now know where he lives, I get to know his habits, his work, his daily life.

London life suits me. Our relationship is like the first day. These two weeks go by too quickly, I'm really happy being with him.

We make plans, we talk a lot. He would like me to stay back and start a live-in relationship but I'm not ready.

And thus starts a life of mutually commuting back and forth for him and for me between Paris and London.

Now I have a man in my life whom I love dearly, although I don't see him very often.

We meet according to our schedules and it doesn't really matter, London or Paris, the main thing is to be together.

My parents consider him as my lover, the chosen one of my heart. They see my happiness in my eyes. They are happy for me.

When he joins me in Paris or sometimes at a work place, we go to a hotel, because I like this lifestyle and it reminds me of our early emotions in Athens.

In London, I stay at his place in Notting Hill. His flat, a typical Victorian house, is on a quiet street with a village atmosphere of the area, Ladbroke Terrace, near Portobello Market.

I lead the life of a housewife with him. I cook for him, wait for him when he comes home from work, beautifully dressed and groomed and smiling.

We sometimes have a drink together like lovers or invite friends, his friends of course, because I don't have a social network here yet.

I am the perfect hostess but I must admit that after a while I miss working. I couldn't stay without having a paid job. I like being independent.

His son comes over sometimes when I'm there, but we don't get along between us is not there. I can't hold him because he screams, runs away from me all the time and only wants to be with his father.

He is over five years old now, he should have got used to me, but no, nothing happens. I'm really the evil stranger who stole his daddy from him.

Will time ease the situation? I can't imagine the day we'll have a child.

Yannis already filed for divorce but it seems to be dragging on. He doesn't talk to me about it, or about his ex-wife. He is silent on the subject and when I ask him about it or whether we will ever get married, he avoids the topic by saying:

- We have time, we'll get married in Greece in the Orthodox Church because I'm not married religiously and that's all that matters to me.

I don't know what to think, but our love is stronger than a piece of paper, even though deep down I dream of carrying his name.

And thus, a full year goes by that seems to me to be just a month. Time has flown so fast.

Then a certain routine sets in. Yannis starts insisting that I move to London and wants me to do so. Its unthinkable for me to start from scratch by making my modelling career here, even though I am a recognised professional. Besides, leaving Paris, my family, my friends and my job would be heartbreaking.

I am more and more in demand and am earning a good living, so why leave for the unknown, even with the man of my life? For him, a true Mediterranean, the woman stays at home.

Am I ready for a real family life? I'm not sure, I still see myself as a little girl, as Yannis keeps calling me. I'm so surrounded, even a bit adored, that I'm still immature for some things in life.

We talk a lot about having a baby and start building castles in the air. He would like a daughter who looks like me and that sets us off into our dreams. But that's not on the agenda for me, at least not yet.

Once my period is delayed and that really gets me into a panic. I tell him about it and I see in his eyes an intense excitement.

- Oh, that would be so wonderful, little girl, a baby from you!

But it's a false alarm and he is bitterly disappointed.

In spite of arguments due to our separations, our love is still very much alive and each visit is as strong as the first day.

*

The years pass commuting between Paris and London.

Summer is coming and I have not accepted any contract for July and August because we have planned to go to Greece and to get married, something I have been really looking forward to for a long time.

That's it, Yannis is finally divorced and we decided to be united in the church in Athens in a small group, his parents and his friends.

From my side, I have only invited Christophe and nobody else because he was the witness of our meeting.

I told my parents about it but they prefer to leave us alone and won't attend the wedding.

I have waited so long for this moment that I want to live through it without a crowd around me, to savour this event intensely.

We have now been in Athens for a fortnight and are staying at the hotel which witnessed the early moments of our blossoming romance.

We asked for the same room to bring us good luck and relive our first love.

It is very hot that year. Yannis goes to see his parents every day but I don't. He had introduced me to them several years earlier but I think they never quite accepted me.

*

Daniel's mother calls them often and they are close to her. Moreover, she bore them their grandson, so she has all the rights. I'm sure they see me as the one who stole their son and destroyed his marriage, the bitch.

I've had the wrong role from the start. They are distant with me and as they only speak Greek, communication is impossible.

I'm getting to understand a little of this beautiful language, but Yannis always discouraged me from learning it. I am frustrated about not being able to speak Greek. I should have ignored it or even learned it on the sly. That would have enabled me to communicate, but that's the way it is.

We met with the priest for the wedding and prepared for the ceremony. It will take place in a week's time in a small church by the sea in Vouliagmeni. Afterwards we will go on a honeymoon to the Cyclades by boat. A friend of Yannis is offering us his yacht and crew for ten days.

Christophe is expected to arrive in three days with my gown, which he got designed and stitched by one of his friends, a promising young couturier, Roland Chessel. Of course, I trust him completely.

It's made of silk chiffon, in a pure ancient Greek style. I will adorn my head with a floral wreath but there will be no veil.

The meal will take place in a traditional Greek tavern in the Athenian countryside with typical dishes.

A simple but chic wedding.

Yannis goes out every night with his friends and is spending his last days of bachelorhood.

As for me, I'm resting at the hotel. I'm tired and nauseous, probably due to stress, so I prefer to remain in a quiet place so that I'm in good shape for the day.

I've already experienced this discomfort before when I was anxious so I'm not worried. It's normal for me to be overcome by these emotional problems.

Yannis comes home during the early hours of dawn and still in a drunken state, but I forgive him and understand.

He is in his own country, with his friends with whom he shares his joy. I am not jealous because I know his love for me. Besides, he proves it to me every night by uniting with me while waiting to take me as his wedded wife at the altar before God.

Only two days left. Christophe has arrived and we have a lot of laughs about everything. The dress is absolutely gorgeous, Roland Chessel is really an upcoming couturier who has a future in the fashion world. In fact, a few years later, I walked the catwalk for him.

I look like a Greek goddess… Am I not Artemis? I strut around in front of the mirror and repeat:

- I am Mrs B. That's me.

And there we go laughing all over again.

On our wedding eve, Yannis and I spend the day together as lovers. We stroll past the places that are familiar to us. Cars honk at us, we are such a beautiful couple, a handsome and tall man looking like a Greek god and me like a diaphanous, blond Nordic goddess.

We are always complimented when we go to a shop or a restaurant.

The day goes by quickly, too quickly, tomorrow I will finally be his wife, above all religiously united with him, which is what really matters to him.

I am living a daydream. I am too lucky. I fear that all this might suddenly come to an abrupt end, but I am not superstitious. Everything is too good. I am on a cloud of happiness.

The last evening is reserved for Yannis' bachelor party with all his friends and also Christophe, who has been invited.

Before leaving for the party, Yannis makes love to me as he has never done before, telling me that he adores me and that I am the woman of his life.

Once he leaves, I go to bed because I am suddenly overcome with fatigue. I fall into a restless sleep. I wake up around midnight still feeling nauseous, I don't feel well, I hope that tomorrow all this will be over!

I turn on the TV to pass the time. I'm not sleepy any more so I wait for the man I love to come back.

It's two a.m. and normally, he comes home around that time.

At three o'clock there is still no sign of him and I start worrying. I call Christophe's room but there is no answer.

At four o'clock, still no news.

They must be really celebrating. In what state will I find him? Completely broken down, soaked in alcohol. He's not going to be fresh for the ceremony, but he's right, let him enjoy himself.

At five o'clock the receptionist calls me:

- Madam, can you come downstairs? The police is here.

My heart starts beating wildly. I rush downstairs, to be greeted by two policemen.

- Madam, you are Yannis B's fiancée.
- Yes, what's going on? I'm worried.
- They had a car accident, they're all in hospital.
- Oh my God, but they are alive?

He dodges the question:

- You have to hurry up, we'll take you there.

The car speeds through the streets of Athens.

Finally, we are at the hospital. The doctor receives me immediately and updates me on Yannis' condition.

He was sitting in the front passenger seat, and was thrown out of the car. His condition is critical and we can't do anything for the moment. Luckily the others got away with light bruises.

- But can I see him?
- Yes, I'll take you to his bedside now.

Yannis is lying there like a puppet, his eyes bloated and his body bruised and lacerated.

I go over to him and take his cold hand.

- Yannis, my love, it's your little girl.

No response.

I kiss his face, his lips, which I so much like to devour, are frozen.

- My love is me.

His eyes open with difficulty, he looks at me. He wants to speak but nothing comes out, he stares at me. Our gazes drown in each other.

- My love, I love you, I would die for your love. Tomorrow we are getting married and I will be your wife forever.

His eyes flash for a moment, his lips part slightly as if to tell me something. A sound comes out that I interpret as "love" and then his hand lets go of mine and he goes on a long journey.

I scream out loudly and faint in a pool of blood. Yannis is dead and so is the child I was expecting.

In-between two phases
I wonder about my life

The tragedy I experienced years before comes back to mind. I must not think about it, especially on this wedding day when I must be happy.

I look out of the window, pensive, my eyes far away drowned in the clouds, my eyes misty with tears that burn me.

I think of Him and our Child, both gone and yet very much present in me.

They are still very much alive in my heart and body. I cannot block them out. They are part of my soul.

My life changed on that cursed day of the accident and on the eve of our wedding. I lost everything: the dream of a life, of a family, gone in an instant.

Everything went very fast and the rest of my life after that was insipid and dull.

*

I'm on tranquillizers. I am sometimes delirious and cry incessantly, hiccupping the name of Yannis.

Christophe, who came out of the accident without a scratch, doesn't let go of me for a moment. He is like a crutch for me because I am unable to live, to react.

I don't even remember the funeral, except that the priest who was supposed to perform our marriage directed the funeral mass.

I am extinct, lifeless and nothing matters to me any more. All I want is to die and join Yannis.

Since the burial, his parents have not spoken to me at all and certainly hold me responsible for their son's death.

They have always been against our relationship and were not looking forward to this marriage. They don't like me, they never did, but who cares, the man I love is dead and my life is destroyed.

I don't belong here any more. Christophe decides it's time for me to go back to France.

In Paris, my parents welcome me with tenderness. It's good to be back in the family circle and in my teenager's room.

- My dear, get some rest, try to forget it, even if it won't be easy. Your father and I are here and we love you.

Sobbing all along, I stammer:

- I know, Mum, but he's dead and so is the baby I was carrying.

And a torrent of tears flows from my aching eyes.

- Hush my little sweetheart, sleep.
- Mum rocks me like when I was little and I end up falling asleep in her arms.

I wake up in the night screaming. I don't know where I am, and am invaded by nightmares. My mother comes running in, frightened.

- Diane, what is it, dear?
- Oh Mum, it's you! I'm in Paris... I didn't know where I was, I was lost in a horrendous dream.
- Don't worry, you're at home and safe and sound.

The next day, I wake up, all groggy and nauseous.

Good morning my darling, the phone has not stopped ringing for you, Robert, Gerald, Nicolas, Christophe and your friend Birgit.

- How nice, I don't know what to say.

The phone rings, Mum runs to answer it.

- It's Gerald, do you want to talk to him?

I nod and take the phone.

- Gerald, I say in a whisper.
- Diane, how are you feeling now?
- Bad, I'm in pain Gerald.
- I understand, my dear, my heart goes out to you, because you've been through a terrible tragedy. It's like that, you can't do anything about it and you have to pull yourself together.

I listen to his speech without really paying attention to it. He can't understand what I'm going through in my heart. My head is empty and I can't really understand what he's saying.

- Can you hear me, Diane?
- Yes, yes, Gerald, I have to get hold of myself.
- I told Robert about my idea and he thinks it's the best way out for you.
- What idea?
- I've booked you for a show in Belgium in twenty days.
- But I won't be able to make it, you haven't seen me! My looks are not up to the mark and I won't be able to do it, its beyond my capacity.
- Oh yes, you will, and within twenty days you'll get back your looks, you're young and you're capable of doing it. I'll wait for you at the agency the day after tomorrow and we'll talk about it. Love, darling.

And he hangs up without waiting for my answer.

- Mum, Gerald is sending me to Belgium to do a fashion show.
- Oh, that's really good, sweetheart, you need to take pleasure in life again.

Everyone wants to decide for me, and after all, it's better that way. I have no sense of judgement. I don't give a damn for anything.

- I'm going to my room to rest.

Once I'm alone, I pull out the music I used to listen to as a teenager: Mozart and the Gregorian chants that did me so much good at that time.

The music lulls me and I plunge into a kind of meditation that takes me to the Tibetan heights.

I feel good, a kind of peace invades me and tells me that life must go on.

I let my thoughts invade me, I listen to them telling me what I have deep down inside me.

I gradually let myself calm down in the darkness of my room and of my heart.

Yannis will continue to remain the man of my life, my ideal, my duplicate.

Will I ever experience something like this again, this togetherness, this fusion, this love? Only the future will tell.

It's my duty to continue living in his memory, perhaps to fall in love again, to have a child.

I drag my feet to go to my agency with an unwillingness that retains me at each step, but I have to move, to get out of my lethargy.

- Hello everybody, Gerald is not in?

- Sure, he is, he'll be back in fifteen minutes Diane, says Vivian, an American woman.
- Sit down, do you want a coffee?
- No thanks, I'll be fine.

I am lost in thoughts when Gerald comes in and startles me.

- Diane, my dear! Let me take a look at you. You've lost weight, but it suits you.
- Well, you look a bit pulled down, but you'll improve as time goes by.
- So you're ready for Belgium? To Liège to be exact.
- Yes, if you like. And what's this job about?
- Simple, it's our partner agency that also has a school and is organising its annual year-end competition.
- I see. And what role do I play in here?
- You'll be part of the .jury; you'll be distributing the prize to the winner in a gorgeous evening gown and you'll parade at the end. You will represent France, our agency, our models and all that for 3,000 francs, including travel, hotel, etc. Not a bad job, eh?
- Gerald, you're right, I should start taking up my activities again, but gradually, okay?
- Don't worry, only pleasure and fun.

I don't have to do anything for this new contract, just show up in Liege two days before. So I have plenty of time until I leave, but what do I do at the moment?

I need to keep myself busy because bouts of grief suddenly flare up in my heart without any warning.

And how about going to the hairdresser, just to change my style? But I can't do that without the agency's permission.

As I'm still in the neighbourhood, I rush back to consult Gerald.

- Hello again, it's me!

I go straight to him with a determined step.

- Diane, don't tell me you've changed your mind about your contract...
- Yes, I changed my mind.

I leave him guessing in suspense.

- Oh, no, Diane, it'll do you good to work again.
- I've changed my mind about myself, or rather I want a new face!
- A face! You want to undergo plastic surgery? You're crazy...

This misunderstanding is taking a comical turn.

- No, a new haircut.
- You scared me, I thought you'd lost your mind!

It's not a bad idea, but we need to seek professional advice, let me phone some friends.

He picks up the phone and moves ahead.

That's what I like about him: we don't waste time.

- They will expect you in an hour in their saloon in Saint-Germain-des-Prés, here's the address.

We're all set to see a new Diane, I think it will do me good.

I was expecting a famous saloon like Carita or Alexandre, but no, it's small like an ordinary neighbourhood salon. However, all of them are stylish and fashionable.

- Hello, I'm Diane from the modelling agency, I say to the man who introduces himself to me.
- I'm Yves and I'll be taking care of you. Come, I'll introduce you to the team. My darlings, her name is Diane and I don't need to tell you she's a model, you can see from her looks.

At that point the clients turn around to look at me, but I'm getting used to that.

- This is Patou, my partner, Christian, the hairdresser, Carole, the colourist, and Patricia the manicurist.

- Welcome, Diane, they tell me.

Yves takes me straight to Christian's chair.

- He'll attend to you first, to see what we can do. We'll inform Gerald what we plan to change. After he gives the go-ahead, I'll do your hair. Not a bad programme, my dear!

And he gives me a kiss.

I'm really enjoying being here, to the extent that I even forget my sorrow.

- So let's see, beauty, what we're going to do, says Christian, smiling at me.

And he looks at me from all angles, touches my hair, puts it in all directions and calls Yves.

- Just do a slight trim but emphasise the steps well and lighten the hair with highlights, that's my diagnosis.

- I think you're right; I'll phone the boss straight away.

He comes back a few minutes later.

- Let's start, we've got his green light.

Christian takes charge of me. While he's at work, we start chatting and disclosing a little bit about our lives.

I don't say anything about the recent events and talk more about my job as a model, but he, on the other hand, is discreet about his private life but I can make out he is gay, I see a lot of them now.

I am now experienced in recognizing them and I like their company. They are sincere and I laugh a lot with them.

I gradually see myself being transformed and I think the result won't be bad at all.

After the highlights and the cut, I go to Yves for the styling.

With him too, we open up and share a good chemistry. I even have the impression that he is flirting with me.

He makes tender gestures towards me, talks in my ear and says nice things to me, very nice indeed. I don't really understand because he told me that Patou was his boyfriend, but after my romance with Nicolas, nothing surprises me any more.

Time just flies in their company; the atmosphere is too nice and I am surprised to hear myself laughing. How good it is to laugh!

I have a new face, my expression in the mirror speaks volumes. I am radiant, with a new aura.

A tear flows down my cheek, because Yannis appears in my mind (how he would have loved to see me like this).

Yves sees me crying.

- Diane, you are gorgeous, I hope these are tears of joy that you are shedding.

Not wanting to reveal my true emotions, I reassure him:

- Of course, Yves, I am too beautiful.
- No, not too beautiful, you are beautiful like a goddess.

Upon hearing this word, "goddess", I am taken back to my past in Greece, my friends who used to call me goddess, my meeting with Yannis.

In a flash, everything comes to the surface and I burst into tears in Yves' arms. He holds me like this for a long time, tenderly, whispering sweet nothings to me.

- I love the smell of his lemon perfume and the softness of his skin.

He takes my head and kisses me gently on the lips.

My body tingles at this unexpected and inappropriate contact. I had already forgotten these sensations.

I withdraw from this embrace, I am confused.

- I'm sorry, Yves, but the fatigue and the happiness of seeing myself so beautiful have overwhelmed me.
- Don't say any more, Gerald told me a little about it.
- Oh, I see.
- Would you like to join us tonight for dinner at a new restaurant? Say yes, it would give me such pleasure.

Without thinking, I accept his proposal:
- You can stay here until then, it's already six o'clock. I'll do your hair and Christian will do your make-up, he's an expert.

What a godsend to be in the hands of these really lovely professionals!

Of course, the bun is beautiful and the make-up perfect.

In the end, it makes me feel good to be pampered, it heals old wounds.

The evening in this famous trattoria in the 8th circle of Paris is very pleasant, the Italian food excellent. The hairdressing salon team welcomes me like a friend, asks me about my job, how I started, they want to know everything.

We carry on smoothly in a friendly atmosphere as if we were old friends.

I am sitting between Yves and Christian with Patou in front of us. Throughout the meal, Yves talks in my ear, tells me I'm beautiful, sexy and has fun undoing the bun he made some time before.

I undoubtedly find this gesture erotic and these words whispered into my ear do not leave me indifferent, but what does he expect out of me?

The end of this exquisite dinner ends with an applause because a cake arrives to celebrate a birthday, Patou's birthday.

Everyone had hidden the event from me. I am confused so

instead of a present I cover the lucky celebrant with tons of kisses.

A beautiful evening that ends in good spirits.

As I am leaving, Yves asks me for my phone and says he will call me as he has some things to suggest. In my head, I say to myself "God knows what".

The next day, as predicted, he calls me.

He suggests I come to his and Patou's house to enjoy their terrace and the good weather.

Why not? I say to myself. *They're nice and it will divert my mind a bit.*

So, there I am comfortably installed at their place, sitting on a deck chair and sipping rum cocktail specially prepared for me.

My head starts to spin, it's three p.m. and I haven't eaten much at lunch. We do some light talk about everything and nothing. Yves devotes a lot of attention towards me and really pampers me, whereas Patou is more distant but still very kind to me.

I close my eyes and sink into a lethargic drowsiness. Kisses on my face make me jump, I open my eyes abruptly and see Yves leaning over me.

- Diane, I like you.

I start screaming out:

- Yannis! Yannis!

Yves shakes me gently and takes my head in his hands.

- Diane, I'm sorry, I find you so beautiful, I'm so baffled… But forgive me.

Without saying a word, I get up and leave. At the door I say:

- I like you too, but I can't go through it, my heart is in

pain.

Outside, I take in deep breaths of air and decide to walk home.

Why do men find me attractive, and in particular homosexuals? Why do they want my body? I'm not just that, though. What kind of image am I projecting?

I am lost in thought and cross the street without realizing it. A taxi honks its horn and calls out to me:

- Hey little lady, watch your step!

I blush and apologise.

I was so engrossed in a certain contemplation that carried me to Tibet that I didn't see what was around me.

How nice it would be to find myself in a hermitage and without all these men lustfully eyeing me…

The next day I receive a huge bouquet of roses with a card signed by Yves and Patou with the words:

To our muse Diane, with all our apologies!

At the same time, I get a call and I think it's Yves, but far from it, it's just good old Gerald.

- Diane, the hair salon wants you for their next commercial.

- Which salon?

- Diane, the one that Yves owns! He just spoke to me and is hiring you for their next ad campaign.

Two months later, my poster is displayed on all subway stations and in fashion magazines. I've become their ambassador to promote their hair salon. A great gift from them.

Their meeting allowed me to get back to work and start to forget, a little.

Since then, they have become close friends with whom I spend wonderful moments of laughter and friendship.

Yves hasn't given the idea of making me his mistress, but he's realised that it's never going to happen... certainly never. In fact, he is an eternal seducer and cannot stand being rebuffed.

One day, I blatantly asked him why he wanted to make love to me when that was not really his orientation and he answered frankly:

- I would have liked you to be the one and only woman with whom I had a sexual experience and I genuinely have feelings for you.

These words sounded familiar, as I had already heard this speech from Nicolas. Why me?

*

I'm in the train on my way to Belgium but I don't really feel like it. I accepted this contract, a little to please, so I have to respect it because I am a professional and it is good for my morale.

I try to convince myself, but my heart is not bearing with me.

I go dragging my feet along and my smile disappeared from my face.

Not quite a good image of the French model, they will be disappointed.

On the station platform, a young man holds up a sign with my name. I approach him.
- Hello, I'm Diane.
- Welcome to Liège, Mademoiselle.

And he offers me a bouquet of beautiful flowers. What a formal way to greet, a welcome worthy of a star!

My hotel is fabulous, in the centre of this friendly city. I discover on my bed my timetable with literally an hourly breakdown of each activity.

It's funny, I feel like a public figure, which in the end will turn out to be true.

On studying it more carefully, I see that I have a meeting at the town hall with the burgomaster, the equivalent of a mayor in our country, a dinner with the partners of this event and the big day of the packed fashion show. A busy schedule.

In fact, I'm here representing French fashion in Belgium.

Tonight, however, I have an appointment with the director of the modelling agency.

I have a few hours left to relax and hang out in the suite I'm occupying.

Since Greece, I love staying in hotels, so I immediately get my bearings, occupy the space available by making myself completely at home, and as a matter of fact, I could stay here all the year round.

Time passes so quickly that I don't even notice the time and the concierge calls me:
- Mademoiselle, Mrs D. is waiting for you at the reception.

My God, I'm not ready yet.
- Tell her I'll be there in fifteen minutes.
- Yes, Mademoiselle.

She'll think I'm putting on airs of a diva, I hate being late, what a good start.

I get ready in a hurry, put on a dress, fix my hair but don't put on any make-up, after all, it's not an official moment tonight and I look very cute with my cleanly scrubbed face.

A tall, somewhat stout woman, seeing me arrive, runs towards me with a smile.

- Good evening, I'm sure you're Diane!

And she embraces me.

I am surprised by this first contact, but the woman seems cheerful and friendly.

- Indeed, I am Diane.
- I couldn't be mistaken, you are just like in your photos, beautiful, impressive!

I forgot, my name is Colette.

- Well, we're going to the agency and then to the restaurant, is that all right with you?

Without even waiting for my answer, she takes me by the arm and leads me outside to her car parked in front of the hotel.

She goes on and on talking to me while driving. I feel I'm not in a car but in a speeding train, like this woman. Her logorrhea continues non-stop.

And she tells me her life story, that she used to be a model and that now she runs the school and the modelling agency she created.

The premises are on the first floor of a mansion located downtown, and after a hurried visit, we finally land in her office.

- So, Diane, how about a glass of red wine? I'm dying of thirst.
- Not more than one glass for me.

And she pulls out a bottle of wine from behind her desk, from a cupboard. I can't believe it, I hope I haven't come across an alcoholic, that would be the last straw.

Finally, the wine is very good and her company pleasant. She asks me questions about my life, how I came to be a model.

I answer them with pleasure, quite surprised at myself to

confide in her like this. I am at ease with her and I even tell her my love story. She listens to me without being intrusive and I highly appreciate this discretion.

When the bottle is finished, she decides that we won't go to a restaurant, and she announces that she will prepare a nice Belgian style home-cooked meal for both of us.

The meal is perfect, chicken, French fries, apple compote, a good mix that is new to me.

The evening passes pleasantly eating and taking sips of another bottle of good wine. She is good company, a lively person. We laugh a lot.

She walks me back to my hotel... like going at full speed. I hang on to the door. I go to bed immediately a little tipsy, and fall asleep thinking about the big day ahead of me.

Upon waking up, a good breakfast prepares me to face the battlefield, because it's going to be a long day. A hairdresser has to come to prepare me and I have to be ready by noon.

I'm going to be received at the town hall, so its out of question to miss the call.

The hotel concierge announces the arrival of the hairdresser. Valerie is a plump brunette woman in her forties. She is charming. We sympathise immediately. She tells me she is intimidated that I impress her.
- But Valerie I'm no one special.
- Oh yes! A great model.
- In size, yes!

It makes her laugh.

I put her at ease by telling her exactly what I want.

While it is running, she doesn't talk to me much. The result is not bad at all. But it's still not Yves who is really an expert in the field who knows how to identify which style suits you.

Once she's gone, I hurry up because I'm late.

Daytime make-up but quite heavy, elegant dress simple and not sophisticated, I must represent French luxury. I am the French luxury.

All the clothes and accessories were sent by my agency in advance and there was no room for improvisation.

In fact, everything was waiting for me in my room with instructions to follow.

I am at the reception when Guy, the driver who had picked me up at the station, shows up. He asks me to hurry, we must be on time.

My arrival at the town hall was very formal. An usher guides me to a hall of honour where there are already quite a few people.

Colette is there, having a big discussion with the mayor. They see me looking a bit lost and come towards me.

She kisses me and presents me to the mayor. I'm really embarrassed because I'm not used to this kind of reception, but above all, I don't see why I'm entitled to all this fuss.

All that I want that it should be over quickly.

After the introductions, the ceremony begins. The mayor makes a speech about the French-Belgian friendship, the importance of it and the honour of welcoming French fashion that I represent.

Its then Colette's turn to take the microphone. She thanks me for my presence and announces the event that will follow in the afternoon will still be hosted by Diane, the famous French model.

I can't believe my ears, what rubbish! As long as I don't have to talk... As if she had read my mind, at the end of her speech, she hands over the microphone to me.

Oh my God, what a shame, what a trap! I've never spoken in public and I don't know what to say.

I think quickly and, in a whisper, I say this utterly stupid sentence:

- Thank you for this welcome and I look forward to seeing you all this afternoon at the Grandes Galeries, where I will parade to my great pleasure and I hope yours too.

A thunder of applause resounds and flashes of photographers blind me.

Its like the Cannes film festival but in Belgium.

Deep down I can't take it any more but I have to continue smiling. The whole thing ends with an aperitif where I have to give answers to all these people I don't know and who imagine I'm someone important.

Phew, it's over, I have three hours left before the next part.

Colette wants to invite me to the restaurant but I refuse, I need to be alone.

I ask her to take me back to the hotel and to pick me up later.

Once in my room, I lie down and sink into a deep and agonizing darkness.

I am being chased by a horde of people who worship me. I don't know how to escape them.

Finally, I pass through a door and find myself in the Himalayan mountains. I breathe and am saved.

I wake up sweating and still full of this oppressive nightmare. Once again, Tibet saves me.

I have an hour before the rest of the day. I soak in a warm

bath and let my imagination run wild.

I let myself go, which in fact I will learn much later by practicing meditation.

I'm ready when Colette comes to pick me up.

As compared to our French department stores, Les Grandes Galeries of Belgium is the shop which is, I would say, between the BHV and the Galeries Lafayette in France.

On the first floor, a whole space has been set up for the event. A podium has been erected in the middle of the hall, where the fashion show will take place. In front of it is a table and chairs for eight people.

I ask Colette:

- Why this table?
- For the jury, Diane.
- The jury for what?
- The jury for the graduation of the students from my school and you are an honorary member.
- My God, I've never done that before, Colette!
- Don't worry, you'll do fine. You'll march in before the results are announced and you'll give the excellence award to the one who stands first.

I don't answer anything, I'm speechless.

Everything is going very fast; I am tutored by the professional team like a star.

Everyone is very considerate towards me, just as it was a few hours earlier.

Do they really think I am so important, even famous?

But France has such a prestigious image abroad that out here we all shine with an aura.

At the table, I am surrounded by journalists, a former Miss Belgium, the shop manager, Belgian models and Colette.

The local press is present and the crowd has invaded the space.

So, I represent the jury. We write down our comments on cards and our score.

The girls introduce themselves one by one. I can see that they are nervous, I would not like to be in their shoes.

I was lucky enough to have been spotted without having any intentions of becoming a model.

Whereas they have a dream and it's all going to be decided now. I must say that some of them don't have the profile at all, too small, too fat, but they want it, they believe in it and that's good.

I'm going to change while the results are being counted.

Now, the decision has been taken.

In the end, I'm not required to parade because we are late, but I have to name the first three winners. Apparently, I have been sent here only to represent the fashion world.

I take my role seriously, dressed in an evening gown by the designer Loris Azzaro, and I enjoy it. The winner is a pretty brunette whom I had given the first score. My choice was not so bad and I had a good sense of perception.

We are photographed, we are applauded and everyone is happy.

The next day, while leaving, I see myself on the front page of the local newspaper with the headline: "Famous Parisian model lights up the city of Liege".

I buy several newspapers and read it in the train. I laugh to myself at this futility, but I have the impression that people need to dream and to identify themselves.

Travelling and getting back to work has done me a lot of good and has helped to heal my sorrows. I'm happy to have accepted this contract, which gets me moving again.

I am healing slowly because the wound is still raw and if I am happy inside, the wound is nevertheless very much there.

The nights are sometimes difficult, I wake up with a start, shouting "Yannis". Time will certainly ease my suffering. That is life.

*

Having survived for the next two years, I continue my life as a model. I live with my parents because I don't have the courage to live alone, to face my demons still very much present in me.

I haven't completely wiped out this chapter from my mind. Will it happen one day?

In the meantime, I go through life like puppet who is a bit broken up from the inside, on the surface beautiful and smiling, but deep down all befuddled in happy but still painful memories.

I go out, see friends, my social life is fully booked but I' missing something… someone.

Nicolas is very much present, and plays the role of a knight in shining armour. He is always available for me.

Our relationship has become like an old couple, we are very close, we understand each other without speaking. He does me good.

Yves and Patou are still my hairdressers and also close friends, I am even closer to Yves, to whom I finally gave in.

I became his mistress one evening during a weekend in Deauville with friends.

I wanted to feel like a woman again in the arms of a man and maybe forget the one who was always haunting me.

Since that night, he is the only man who touches my body, with the blessing of his companion. I love him in my own way and this situation suits me, I don't have to commit myself, and neither does he.

I am a bit of a muse for him, he tells me, and a muse is loved.

He is the only man who has touched me physically since Yannis, I am still faithful to his memory. Yves is different, he's a homosexual. Or rather bi, apparently.

I've matured in my head; the trials of life make me think more. I question myself about my future, Tibet is still in my thoughts for me and in me.

I am starting to learn more about Buddhism, it is anchored in my body, I don't know why.

As for my body, it does not change, I still look younger than my age despite all these years.

And time passes.

A contract takes me to Switzerland to parade in a department store. I know Switzerland because I took part in winter sports over there as a child. I loved this country with its beautiful mountains and landscapes.

I am happy to go there. Little do I realise at that time that Switzerland will become my future home.

As in all the foreign countries where I have worked, I am welcomed like a queen, the prestige of France still makes an impace.

The team is nice, both the models, hairdressers, make-up

artists and the people in the shop.

As I mentioned earlier, being a French model opens doors for you, especially as the trend for supermodels is slowly coming. I'm pampered, I'm asked my opinion on everything.

The other models ask me questions about Paris, they all dream of the catwalk, of the great couturiers, of posing for fashion magazines.

I answer kindly, give them tips and addresses. When I think that it was so easy for me…

We parade for women's and men's fashion; three male models are with us.

I particularly like one of them, Philippe.

I do three runs with him as well as the final in a wedding dress.

We are well matched and look as if we're made for each other, it shows on our faces.

I am there for three days, and Philippe offers to show me the city and its nightlife.

The same evening, he invites me to an Italian restaurant in the village of Carouge, a typical Sardinian neighbourhood south of Geneva.

The waiter recognises us and tells us that he saw us in the afternoon at the fashion show.

This situation gives me a strange feeling of a *déjà vu* and makes me feel.

I'm reliving the evening spent in Paris with Nicolas, except that we are in Geneva several years later.

Is this a sign?

Afterwards, we go for a drink at the bar of a very chic hotel and we spend the night at the Griffith, the best trendy nightclub in town.

We get on famously and dance like crazy.

He wisely walks me back to my hotel and kisses me tenderly on the cheek, he didn't dare go any further, could he also be like Nicolas?

The next day, at work, we are happy to see each other again. I have a little twinge in my heart when I see him.

I haven't experienced this since Yannis, I don't know what to think.

He suggests that we go out again tonight, I agree because the next day is my last day and I will be going back to Paris. Also, I undoubtedly desire to spend more time with him.

The evening is a success and this time he takes a step forward. I feel good with him and end up in his arms.

He lives in a charming duplex in the old town, like Nicolas, another point in common. Like Nicolas, he is tender, considerate, attentive to me, to me and to my body, which has been dormant for so long.

The day has already dawned and the sun's rays that pierce through the shutters caress my face.

I catch a glimpse of a figure leaning over me and whispering my name, I wake up slowly and smile at him.

- Diane, breakfast is ready, we have to hurry, we need to be at work in two hours to get ready, today the first show is at two p.m.

- Yes, Nicholas, I say, smiling at him again.

At the same time, I realise what a blunder I've made. Oh my God, how do I make up for it and what do I say?
- I'm sorry Philippe, I was still asleep.
- It's okay, Nathalie.

I look at him with surprise and we both burst out laughing at the same time.

He reminds me so much of Nicolas that I confuse the first names, but he is intelligent and reacted with humour.

The afternoon is absolutely magical, we laugh all the time and it makes an impact on our work, we are applauded a lot, especially at the end, when we parade in wedding dresses.

The contract in Switzerland is over and Philippe offers to accompany me to the airport. I don't want to leave him. How will this story end again?

The farewell is sad, he asks me to come back as soon as possible. A small tear kisses my cheek as I cross the border.

Will I see him again?

I have hardly put my luggage down at home when the phone rings.
- Diane, it's for you, my mother shouts.
- Hello, I say in a slightly annoyed tone.
- Diane, it's Philippe.
- Oh, Philip, it's you, I've just arrived.
- I miss you so much, Diane, I couldn't wait to hear from you.
- That's so sweet… But let me get settled and call me back in an hour, I'll be free to talk, I miss you too.

I don't know what to think, I do miss him, but to what

degree, I don't realise it yet. I'm still so burnt with love for Yannis that I can't see myself with a man.

What to do? What to say? Where to go? What is my life?

Spiritually Yours
Listening to My Soul

After searching for our way, we finally arrived at the Karma Ling Monastery, perched at 1,200 metres in the mountains between Chambéry and Grenoble in France. Martine, my colleague who is with me, is accompanying me on my first visit to a Buddhist centre.

I am really moved, its been so long that I have been looking for a place where I could discover this philosophy! Because in my opinion, it is not a religion.

The place is incredible, hidden in a green setting, bordered on one side by a river and on the other by a lush forest.

The centre is housed in the thirteenthcentury Carthusian monastery. I am impressed when we pass through the front door, I feel unsuspected energies that disturb me. I lower my voice to speak, as if I were in a church.

- How serene it is! I whisper to Martine.

At the reception desk, all the formalities for our stay and our internship are explained to us, but we have to hurry and have lunch first, because it is lunchtime.

Lunch is served in the temple because it is a week of silence.

We enter and I am shocked. The hall is beautifully decorated in the Tibetan Buddhist style with a huge Buddha enthroned in all its splendour.

They make signs to tell us to sit on cushions in front of small red tables.

Sitting cross-legged is not easy for a Westerner and I am not used to it.

I look at Martine and smile at her, letting her know that I am not comfortable.

A prayer is said which I find very beautiful, even if I don't understand anything, then we are served food.

Eating in silence is difficult, I would like to express myself, to share my thoughts with Martine, but it is impossible.

The positive side is that you taste what you have on your plate, that it gets better and above all that you take your time.

I am delighted, I am in heaven, I am finally here, at home. Everything speaks to me, smiles at me, dazzles me, I have reached home.

The course introduces me to the precepts of Buddha. I discover his philosophy. I learn the teaching called Dharma and I am now part of a community: The Sangha.

We are awakened at six o' clock by a gong which announces the morning meditation.

Still asleep, we go to the temple where we meet, recite mantras and meditate.

How good I feel and in harmony with my being!

Everything is done in a group, breakfast, lunch and dinner, all in silence.

In the morning and afternoon, we have an introduction to Buddhism with a lama.

I finally discover what I have wanted to do since I was a teenager. I am not disappointed; my dream is coming true.

The exchange between the participants is fruitful because everyone is interested in learning more.

After the course, we go for a walk in the surrounding forest, to recharge our batteries near the river.

I vibrate during the meditations with the chanted mantras, I empty my mind. My body aches because the cross-legged position does not suit me, but I am happy to continue.

The three days have gone by at a hectic pace but so positive that I want to come back as soon as possible.

We are now on our way back to Geneva. The return to civilization is strange, we had totally disconnected from everyday life.

- I feel like I've been away for a month, I say to Martine.
- So do I, she says. And how good it feels to let oneself go!

I'm glad to be back in my flat, with a new sense of having finally found my real self, with more emphasis on the spiritual aspect than the physical side.

*

I have been living in Switzerland for several years now and more specifically in Geneva.

My romance with Philippe has turned into a stronger feeling and when he asked me to move in with him, to get married, I bluntly said yes without thinking.

I wanted to turn a painful page of my life and continue my journey with someone.

I'm getting married tomorrow, my parents came all the way here because they want to support me, feeling that I am still very vulnerable.

I am already living with my future husband but I have

decided to stay in a hotel for my last night as a single woman. Alone in this room, my whole story comes back to my mind like a boomerang.

I can't sleep. I am anxious, for fear of reliving my tragically unfulfilled marriage in Greece.

I'm afraid the phone will ring and some horrible disaster will be announced to me.

At the break of dawn, I am relieved after Philippe's phone call. He is alive.

We have an ordinary and classic wedding ceremony without any fuss between close family and friends. At the town hall, the ceremony is simple.

I refused a religious union. The only one that would have meant anything to me didn't take place.

When I say "yes", I think of Yannis and I pronounce that word to him.

Yes, now I am his wife… Whose wife? That is the question.

Philippe left modelling to work as a nightclub manager. As for me, I still pursue my work in Switzerland for a while, but the opportunities are less than in France.

I'm starting to get bored. Our time schedules are not the same, he comes home late at night, we are getting out of step and seem to be slowly drifting apart.

After giving it considerable thought, I think of continuing my studies again, but what next?

Unfortunately, I have no idea. I could see myself as an air hostess or a teacher, but I don't have the baccalaureate degree. So what should I do?

Fate does things well. Sometime after my ideas for a change, a friend of my husband's mentions her desire to launch a luxury ready-made boutique to invest her money.

She doesn't want to be present there, and is looking someone to manage it.

Philippe tells me about it and I see myself telling him that I would be interested because I would like to take a different direction in my life.

He is speechless.

- But Diane, you don't have to work, I am earning enough.
- Philip, I'm bored. Talk to your lady friend and tell her I'm interested.
- As you wish, I'll call her tomorrow.

The discussion turns sour. It's impossible have a dialogue with him and he doesn't like conflicts. I don't insist and wait to see if he does what he says.

To my great astonishment, the next day when we meet, he tells me that I have to call for the management of the shop. The deal went through quickly. My husband's friend is delighted to have me as manager.

I really enjoy being the manager of a fashion boutique, I quickly got used to it and Carole, the boss, gave me all my freedom to decide as I wish.

After six months, I already have a clientele that appreciates me, that loves my taste and my choice of clothes. I have such a high turnover that I renew the collection every month.

Of course, my modelling background and all my contacts help me a lot to achieve this success.

I have created a new network of friends with whom I go out and have fun. I feel like I'm living the teenage years I never knew, having been thrust into the adult world overnight.

I am fully aware that I am living in an artificial world, but it seems so deliciously exciting to me during that time of my life.

Almost every night, my girlfriends and I go to clubs, avoiding my husband's club which is too snooty and stilted for us.

It felt so good to laugh and to feel free! I am finally me.

I let myself get carried away in my follies all night long, reaching ultimate heights of revelry and merry-making, and drown myself in these mundane pleasures to forget the unsatisfactory life I am leading.

With Philippe, life is so monotonous... He is immature. He is not the man on whose shoulder I can lay my head.

I made a mistake marrying him. I wanted to escape a past that was still painful. I thought I could forget everything with him, but I can't.

I think I am not happy with him. The shadow of Yannis is still present in my life. I can't help but make comparisons and they don't seem to go in the right direction.

My first wrinkles are appearing, I'm going through a depression that is keeping me nailed to the mast of my life. It's time to curb my feelings and move ahead, otherwise I shall be heading straight towards the wall of death.

I've put on weight and don't recognise myself any more, I say goodbye to the slender model envied by all, and now welcome this new stranger with generous curves. I am now a shadow of my former self.

Just a ghost wandering through a life that is no longer my own.

I can no longer react, being totally drugged by my doctor who takes the easy way out rather than sending me to a psychiatrist. I'm just a zombie dragging myself to work.

One day everything starts moving very fast during a moment of clarity.

Philippe doesn't support me, I don't care about my life. I have to react, react, react.

I decide to take control over my life and ask for a divorce. My husband doesn't understand why, doesn't even discuss it and merely agrees.

During the procedure, I try to get back on track. I go to see a psychiatrist, on my own initiative, who does hypnosis. Incredibly, in one session, I feel better already.

Everything becomes clear. I release what is buried inside me and my whole love story with Yannis explodes in expiatory tears.

I free myself of an immense weight. I had got into a self-created shell within myself, these shapes around me prevented others from approaching me and protected me from reliving my misfortunes.

Finally, I don't like Philippe. I don't like my present life.

My psychiatrist makes me think about myself and my future. He makes me understand that my whole life has been based on my looks and that I only had my beauty to convince.

- It is time, dear lady, to move on.

This sentence hits me like a boomerang. He's right, I was only a decorative figure without a thinking brain.

I am only half of myself. I'm not whole, something is missing within me to really exist, to be someone in my own right.

He advises me to assess my skills and competencies, to enroll at the unemployment office, to explain my situation to them. He drafts a letter explaining my case which is going to be of great use to me.

It is the beginning of another life, a new era.

Life is really segmented in fractions, of good and bad moments, of dreams, of achievements, of failures. The line is not straight, there are twists and turns, black holes, but the sun is always shining at the end, after the storm and happy encounters.

I finally take my life in hand. I am becoming an adult.

It's not easy for me to take all these steps. I have always been guided and projected in the limelight. I have to make an effort, but I realise that I am a fighter and that when I have decided on something, I make it to the end.

Today I have an appointment at the Career Guidance Office of Geneva.

I'm nervous about presenting myself because I can't make any claims to have done any studies and is modelling really a profession?

I feel reduced to the size of a tiny ant that day in front of the counsellor, the funny thing is that she is so short and small that I look like a giant in front of her. Life can be so unpredictable!

I tell her my life story. She listens to me without cutting me short. I just go on and on and it does me good to talk. I unveil everything, from my modelling debut to my divorce and my life in Switzerland.

- What exactly do you want? she asks.
- To change, to change everything.
- Are you aware that it can be difficult and disturbing?
- I think so, but I'm ready, even if I have to struggle with it.
- Well, I'm going to give you a skills assessment and after that I'll be able to guide you more accurately because your life path is complex and not a straight-forward one.

- I'm sure it is.

An appointment is made for the following week for this test.

I go to her on the appointed day, anxious.

- Don't worry, Madam, you just have to answer this questionnaire, it will take you at least an hour because you have to think carefully and not answer in a hurry.

It takes me almost two hours because I'm not used to writing and I have to think about my life, my whole life.

It's a perilous exercise that brings back more or less pleasant events.

I am ashamed that I didn't pursue my studies, even though the school of my life gave me competencies and abilities I did not expect.

These hidden skills should surface from within and guide me to the jobs that would best correspond to me.

I have finished and am relating the end of my life. I sluggishly hand over my paper to the counsellor.

- Here you are, I say simply, in a little girl's voice on the verge of tears.

- Well, we'll analyse it and I'll call you back for the results.

- Very well, Madam. Looking forward to meeting to again soon.

I leave the office, drained out and disgusted. I can't do it, that's for sure.

I want to give up everything, to go away, far away, to Tibet, and live in a very happy plenitude, but life is not that simple.

I return to Philippe's flat where I'm still staying, because we are not yet divorced and he allows me to still live with him.

He is still in love with me and agrees to have me at his place.

He is not there and I relax by drinking a glass of red wine in front of the TV.

I start getting a bit dizzy! Why don't I call my girlfriend Victoria in New York? She lives there now. She's trying to rebuild her life after being a model like me.

Unfortunately, she doesn't answer. I feel rather disheartened, because I badly needed to talk. Well, that's how it is.

I watch TV without really concentrating on it, while dreaming of a happy future.

I'm startled when I hear the phone ring.

- Diane, it's Victoria.
- Oh, my dear, how nice to hear from you!
- For an hour we chat about our lives, our dreams.
- Diane, why don't you come and join me in New York? There's nothing for you to do in Switzerland.
- That's true, I have no more ties here, you're right. I'll come, I say enthusiastically.
- I'll call you back in a few days, my dear, let me think about it.

In my head, everything things start moving very fast. My decision is made. I'm leaving, goodbye Switzerland, goodbye the skills assessment, Philippe. My new life is in the United States.

*

I arrive in New York overexcited but a little dismayed at the idea of not knowing what I am going to experience and discover.

Victoria welcomes me warmly; she is so happy to see me! Her life is also in a real mess at the moment.

She left Paris on a whim due to an infatuation for a rising American model ten years ago.

Now they have parted ways and the problem is that he never wanted her to work. She is now almost homeless and, on the streets, even if I'm exaggerating a bit.

She got a very good pension after her divorce, which allows her to live well, but nothing more. She lives in the middle of Manhattan, a stone's throw from Central Park.

We can't stop talking, telling each other about our memories in Paris, our lives after having been models, but above all about existing in our own right.

We now yearn to unite our mind with our body, making them one integrated whole from now onwards.

Victoria works as a freelancer for a real estate agency.

She projects herself in some sort of a way when she offers flats and tries to rent or sell them. She tells me that she likes this job because she has her own freedom.

I can see that she is doing well, but she certainly lacks something to be really happy. But what is it? Only she knows.

I need a week to get over all these emotions and start thinking about a new life here.

The only snag is that I have a tourist visa and cannot stay here for more than six months.

Until then, I have to find a way to live in the United States and especially find a job, but how do I go about it? I don't know how to do anything except modeling. The choice will be limited. I can only have a basic job.

Its autumn when I get here, and the mild weather enables me to get acclimatized easily to this city, which I find hectic.

The high buildings fascinate me and I often find myself

looking up to the sky, to the infinite.

I think about my past life: where am I at present?

A new path to cross, a renewal, a new life.

I walk around the city with my friend keeping in line her appointments. I explore some of these skyscrapers. I visit flats, especially around the east, south and west side of Central Park.

That's where the most beautiful ones are, but I must admit I'm rather disappointed, they don't have the charm of Paris.

One day, Victoria is all excited.

- I have to flat hunting at Trump Tower and then Central West, and you'll never guess whom the flat belonged to once!
- I give up, I say without looking.
- To Rita Hayworth.

On the way there, we conjure up a whole lot of imaginary fantasies about this actress.

What a disappointment! The flat in Trump Tower is just an empty space without any life to it. I can't visualise myself there, its modern, has a nice view but devoid of all charm.

The star's apartment is in an older building, but small and nothing extraordinary.

That's New York, flashy and superficial, and hasn't lived through the ages.

The characterless walls still don't speak, have little or no history to reveal.

I am nevertheless satisfied at having followed the footsteps of an international star.

Victoria introduces me to a friend of hers who wants to learn French. He is Chinese, and he too is without a work permit, but he has an asset in his favour: he is a feng shui master.

It's the first time I've heard of this ancestral Chinese art: putting the energies together in a place according to various elements.

This is what I understand.

We decide to meet once a week for an hour. I ask him for 25 dollars, which is a lot of money, but I'll get to know about that later.

In fact, the hourly rate for lessons, baby-sitting or a waiter's job is only 10 dollars.

His accommodation is in down town, not far from Chinatown, in a basement.

In all the town hill style houses, people live in these basements. It's modest, gets very little daylight, but its still cozy.

I start by teaching him the alphabet and its pronunciation. There's an ocean of difference between Chinese and French, and he has trouble understanding.

After four lessons, he gives up. Besides, I think it's too expensive. He didn't expect it to be so difficult. His desire was only a dream.

My financial situation is becoming more and more tight, my savings are starting to melt away under my nose.

Life is expensive in New York, especially the rent. I'm a bit worried but I believe in life. If I am here, its undoubtedly to understand something.

Victoria has just rented a flat to an opera singer who will perform at the Met, which is the Metropolitan Opera. She tells him about me because he is looking for someone to look after the flat.

The appointment is made in a beautiful building on South

Central Park.

The tenor is a robust German who is very pleasant. He put some questions on me and hires me without any problem, without really asking me about my skills in this area.

I have to clean and cook dinner every day except on weekends for three hours a day at $25 an hour.

I'm thrilled. I'll be busy and well paid, although it won't be enough to live on.

I start my new job the next day. I laugh as I go because I hate housework.

He is there when I arrive and shows me where things are. The rent is $5,000 a month but I don't find anything extraordinary about the place. Well, it's not my place and it's not his either.

Before I start cleaning, he offers me a cup of tea and we talk. I think he understood that I was a novice in this job.

He decides that I won't do the cooking. For today, he offers to take me to a restaurant. That suits me better, I must say, and I accept.

After cleaning the flat, I sit down with him in a very chic place of a famous hotel.

The situation is funny, the maid and her boss, a real vaudeville, especially as the man seems to show a soft corner for his employee.

I don't dare push him away because I need the job, but I make it clear that he's not my type and we leave it at that.

He is an intelligent man who has a tender inclination towards me. During the two months I work for him, he continues to take me out and introduces me to New York's cultural life, its museums, Broadway and musicals.

I'm absolutely dazzled by the collection of the Frick Museum. I swoon at the sight of the fascinating works on display, especially those by Boucher.

We go to see the stage show of Grease, with Brooke Shields appearing live for the first time, revealing a different side of her talent.

I get the impression that he likes to be seen in public with me, I still have that special Parisian touch that an American does not have.

I continue to apply for other jobs, but the answer is always the same: Green Card, the door opener to stay and work in the United States.

So I settle for my pseudo-housekeeper job but I'm not satisfied, it's not enough to live on, and I'm unable to think any further.

The only positive side is that I am learning to live on little money. I understand that I can do something other than a job that puts me on display, based solely on my looks.

I survive, I live in this lively city that I love, but it's not a long-term solution.

A colleague of Victoria's tells her about a friend of hers who has a stretch limo, those oversized cars. He shows tourists around the city and is looking for someone who knows French for his French-speaking clients.

I'm very much interested. I'm desperate to get a job and earn money. I make an appointment right away; I don't want to miss this chance.

After more than a quick interview with the boss, I immediately find myself a hostess guide in New York.

The boss barely interviews me and I'm hired straight away.

I have to inform my opera singer about this, because unfortunately I won't be able to cope with both jobs, though it would have helped me cope financially. I have to be available for this new job.

He's happy for me, as the end of his contract at the Met is coming to an end, so my withdrawal was well timed.

I need to know the entire history of the city, the geographical location of the districts and their peculiarities so that I can show them and answer visitors' questions. I am absolutely thrilled about what I'm starting to learn about New York and see it differently.

Dan, the owner, a black American from North Carolina who acts as the driver, tells me not to worry, that he will prompt me as I go along if I cannot provide some information.

The first customers are a group of Canadians. I feel terribly nervous but don't show it. I greet them outside the limousine and suddenly get hooked. I am a flight attendant.

- Welcome to the VIP tour!

I am seated behind the driver and the customers are in front of me, six seats are available. A bar is to my left and I serve soft drinks.

It starts off well. I like this job, I feel comfortable. And yes, I am projecting myself!

The tour goes wonderfully well, without a hitch. Luckily Dan is there to give me all the necessary professional information, because I don't know this city after all.

I discover it at the same time as the passengers, but of course without revealing my ignorance.

After three visits, New York holds no secrets for me and I am proud to show it to these tourists.

They think I'm a real New Yorker and I don't deny it when they ask me if I'm American.

- No, I'm French, but I've lived here for a very long time.

What a boastful show-off I am!

*

The problem with these tours is that the income doesn't enable me to live decently. I'm barely able to make both ends meet and am running short of cash for everything now.

I'm stressed out and can't sleep. I don't know what to do any more. I have to take a decision.

Everything is rushing downwards, finances, little work and the worst thing is that my visa is coming to an end. I have three weeks more to decide on a survival strategy.

Either I stay on and join the gang of illegal citizens, or I go back home with my hands in my pockets and head hanging down, with no future ahead of me.

With Victoria, during an evening while sipping a glass of Californian red wine, we discuss the issue again. In the end, Victoria advises me to go back home to be on the safe side.

But where to go, to France or to Switzerland?

I phone my ex-husband and explain the situation.

- Diane, come back, the doors of my house are open to you as long as you want, you're at home here.

The American chapter is now over. I am turning a page in my life. Will I see again the country that taught me to be a new Diane? It taught me that I can live on more than my looks and that money is secondary.

Here I am again, back in Switzerland, no doubt with a roof over my head, but nothing except an uncertain future.

Philippe is adorable and welcomes me with love. He listens to me attentively, something which he had never done before.

I see friends again, everyone advises me to take over a boutique, but I don't feel like it any more.

I keep going over my future in my head, backwards and forwards, to the point of dizziness and anxiety.

I have to act, react and not let myself get down. I am a fighter. In one of these moments of darkness and light, my thoughts carry me back to the career counselling office that I had dropped.

Why not contact them again? I have nothing to lose, and I already passed their tests.

From then on, everything starts moving very fast. The warrior machine that I can be is back in action.

The same counsellor sees me. I explain my situation, that I needed to leave, to take stock, that I was lost.

She understands, she tells me, and it's never too late.

She pulls out the results of my skills assessment and explains to me in detail what it's all about.

The ideal for me is: the social profession.

I am speechless.
- And what do I do then?
- Start all over again.
- Ah, from scratch…
- Yes, nothing is easy in life, but I'm here to help you with

your steps, if you're ready, of course.
And I hear myself saying:
- Yes, it's time, I'm ready.

Mireille is one of those encounters that make you move forward in life and who are there to show you show you which direction to take, like an angel guiding you towards the right path.

Obviously after that, it's up to us to stay on course and not go astray.

Mireille and I are friends now, I thank her and the others who helped me to see more clearly the direction I was taking.

After that, everything moved very fast one after another, with obstacles, happiness, new encounters, a return to school, diplomas were obtained... the beginning of a new life.

Finally, I got my head and my body together.

*

I've been working for a year now in an MJC, as they say in France. I am a cultural and social coordinator. I am in charge of cultural events and young people in difficulty.

I am successful in my job and it's a pleasure to come to the centre every day.

In addition, I a hidden passion for French suddenly surfaces in me; I cannot deny that I had a good level at school.

I therefore draft all the documents and correct the mistakes of my colleagues who have spelling problems.

Once I remember using the term *'par-devers toi'* meaning "in your possession" in French.

All eyes are focused on me, surprised to hear this term they don't know.

- Diane, you're a real Frenchwoman, we've never heard the word *'par-devers toi'* before.

Just like you to pull out words like that!

From now on, I'm not asked to be beautiful but to be intelligent and thoughtful.

The first event I have to organise is a two-week cultural theme event. I start racking my brains because it will be the first time for me, and that's not so easy.

Some ideas do come to mind but I don't think they are relevant; they seem like old clichés. I need something striking to establish myself in my new position.

I sleep over it, and suddenly a flash of inspiration comes in the morning.

But, by golly, as the inspector whose name I've forgotten would say: Tibet. But of course, Tibet.

My proposal is accepted straight away and they think its unique. I have three months to organise everything.

I worked hard, I made contacts, I met people who have contacts with Tibet as well as Tibetans. I'm lucky that there is a large community from this country staying in Switzerland.

I am delighted, at last I am approaching my unattainable dream from the tips of my fingers, my deepest desire and Buddhism, because Tibet is inseparable from this philosophy/religion.

The event that I call "*A few steps on the roof of the world, Tibet*" is a magnificent success that even the Geneva press comments on.

I have coordinated everything well; everything has been well thought about and planned. I put Tibet in the spotlight with songs, dances, conferences, meetings with Tibetans, food stalls with Tibetan dishes, all this taking place in an atmosphere with Tibetan decorations.

The success of this event makes me proud of myself.

Les Amis du Tibet (The Friends of Tibet), a Swiss sponsorship association, is present to make its projects known. I learn about their wonderful work helping child refugees in India.

While talking with them, I realise that I need to take action too, that it is time to get involved. I commit myself to sponsoring a child.

That is how some time later, Ngawang Jampa, a seven-year-old boy, comes into my life.

I receive his photo and a kind of identity paper.

I learn that he had just arrived from Tibet and that he was born on 20 July 1990 in the Kham region. He really has an Asian face, with slanted eyes, a round head and a surprised look.

I am impressed. I touch his photo. I talk to him, tell him about my love for his country, which I don't know but which has been in my heart since I was a teenager.

He is my link now with Tibet, I promise myself I will never break it. I have hoped for this moment so much!

I pay a few dozen Swiss francs to the association each month, which allows my godson to receive an education, to eat, to dress and to remain in Tibetan culture.

Everything is organised by the Swiss organisation and I must admit that everything is done with utmost transparency.

Sometime after the first written message, I receive a letter from India. A nice drawing by Ngawang Jampa is sent to me with a note from the TCV, the Tibetan Children Village, explaining the life of my godson.

I am very touched by this exchange. I do not regret having embarked on this beautiful adventure.

Throughout my involvement, I will continue to receive news from the TCV and Ngawang Jampa three times a year.

I am now well settled in my new professional life.

I love what I am doing. I haven't forgotten my modelling past, but I'm keeping quiet about it. I never talk about those years or about the love of my life, Yannis, and the child I lost.

In the eyes of society, I'm merely an ordinary divorced woman without children like so many others.

Through the sponsorship association I get to know about a Tibetan monastery on Mont Pèlerin, above the Lake of Geneva in Switzerland, and also one in France, between Chambéry and Grenoble.

I gather all this information with excitement and immediately make further inquiries.

On the phone, I can't believe my ears. I am told that the Dalai Lama is coming to give a Buddhist teaching under the direction of Karma Ling, the French monastery.

I want to go, oh yes! I really do! I can't miss this event. With whom could I go?

I immediately think of Mireille, my guidance counsellor, who is always interested in this kind of experience.

Two months later, we are in Pontcharra, France, where the meeting and teaching are being held.

Mireille and I are elated to be there.

A huge tent has been erected on a field, with a no-nonsense and serene atmosphere, without any hustle and bustle.

We go inside and sit on the ground; a platform is placed before us. I feel in perfect harmony with the different people present.

And there he arrives, there is a pin drop silence, an undeniable respect floats in the air. He is there, in front of me, in front of us.

I get chills, what generates from him is indefinable. I feel like crying, I am so overwhelmed.

Him… the Dalaï Lama… in front of me… in flesh and blood. *A dream?* No, a reality!

His teaching lasts two hours. It is translated by Matthieu Ricard, a Buddhist monk of French origin.

I take notes, every word has a meaning for me. I recognise myself in what he says.

Time passes so quickly while listening to him that it this first session has already come to an end.

As he leaves, he glances at the audience and greets them. His eyes roam around the room and I am sure it is me he is looking at.

I'm going to faint. His eyes land on me and run through my whole being with an indestructible happiness.

I am touched by grace, the Catholics would say. Yes, touched by grace, but Buddhist.

His presence is unique, he exudes such empathy and gentleness… This is certainly what being a bodhisattva is all about.

The afternoon is also magical. I only have eyes for him and I literally drink his words. I don't miss a single crumb.

Everything strongly reinforces my wish to become a Buddhist.

My teenage desires were real and not a utopia.

The day goes past at an unimaginable speed. It's already time to go home. I wish I could stay and meet him, that he would give me the key to his compassion. Maybe one day?

We leave, Mireille and I, haloed by his divine presence. We replay the film in reverse, listening again to what touched us, what he said.

For me, the first thing that I recollect is that everything is impermanence, undergoes changing and is inconstant. I make this my motto. According to Buddha, attachment to impermanent things turns out to be the cause of suffering because what is impermanent cannot be satisfying.

Impermanence is also a promise for change: progress on the spiritual path is only possible because, like everything else, our unawakened state is impermanent.

I embrace this principle hundred per cent.

I have entered into what I wanted for a long time with my feet firmly on the ground. I have approached a philosophy that speaks to me and is within me now.

I know that there will be a long path to reach a level of perfection and understanding, but I will get there.

When I return, I tell everyone about it. I annoy some people with my enthusiasm. The Dalai Lama is not yet as well-known as he is today, and to some he could appear to be part of some sect.

But I know that I must follow him, that he is an extraordinary person and that one day he will be recognised as a saint.

One day, while talking to my ex-sister-in-law Florence, she tells me that she would like to return to India, a country she had visited a year ago. She knew that I was sponsoring a child and suggested I accompany her next time to go and meet him.

What a windfall! After a year of sponsoring, I can now have the opportunity to actually go and meet him. We can get to know each other and perhaps create a strong bond.

I jump at this offer with enthusiasm. We decide to leave in February until mid-March for a trip that will take us from the south to the north of India.

For a month and a half, I will get a glimpse of this culture dating back to thousands of years, see where Ngawang Jampa lives and pursue my quest for knowledge.

The highlight for me will be my visit to Dharamsala, where the Dalai Lama and my godson live. I know for sure that I will meet one of the two.

*

I am on the plane that is taking Florence and me towards our Indian destiny.

I am excited about this trip. I don't know Asia at all and frankly, India wasn't really a country that particularly attracted me, but apparently it was written in my destiny that one day I would step foot over there.

We are sitting next to a young Swiss man with whom we get acquainted.

He is going to join his sweetheart in Calcutta who is doing a nursing course with Mother Teresa.

As we chat with him, we realise that we are travelling the

same route as he is.

Arrival in Bombay, then the next day in Calcutta, like us. We decide to continue our journey together, which comforts me.

Having a male guide in this gigantic subcontinent seems to me a good idea.

The flight with him is most pleasant and when we land in India, he takes charge of everything.

After passing through immigration, he leads us towards the exit. He has studied everything and knows what to do. We take a pre-paid taxi to Colaba, the area where all the foreigners gather.

We are outside, very tired from the journey, with our suitcases, in front of the Arabian Sea and near the gateway to India, looking for a hotel, or rather he is looking for one.

We want to rest before going to discover this sprawling city, but not just anywhere.

I need a minimum of comfort.

My first Indian shock erupts when I see the room he has found.

- Oh my God, I don't believe it, I say in amazement.

I take it upon myself because this is only the beginning of our journey and I can't start making a fuss and putting on airs. I have to forget my principles, my luxurious life as a model in palaces.

Now I am someone else and I have to face this new existence.

The only furniture in the room consists of two plain beds without any cupboard to put our things in, but there is nevertheless a shower in a tiled corner and the toilet outside.

This was my first mixed-up impression of India, but one that

I would eventually overcome with the habit of coming here.

Outside, despite the crowds, I feel good vibes in this city. I am comfortable and the poverty, which is said to be all-pervading, does not bother me a bit.

Everything is mixed here, but the differences don't stand out. The multitude of skin colours of the people, their clothing, the dilapidated buildings or the luxury of some hotels form a real kaleidoscope that does not hurt my eyes.

I love these smells, these colours, this mixture of good and bad scents, from incense to faeces, the spices contained in the dishes sold at street corners, which rise up to your nose and throat.

I find myself enjoying this uncertain blend of contrasts that is deliciously tasty at the same time.

You have to be careful where you walk and when crossing the street, because between the sacred cows, the people and the cars, it is a dangerous labyrinth and life is merely dangling on a thread.

*

Calcutta awaits us the next day. Its entirely another world that surprises me.

The city, the people and the architecture are different from Bombay. I think I am in another country.

Here again, we look for a more or less suitable accommodation in the backpackers' street.

Hadrien, our Swiss friend, is still there for us. He finds us a nicer room than in Bombay, with a real bathroom and toilets. Oh, *la la*! What a luxury!

We are here for three days and we are determined to see as

much as possible and especially to go to Mother Teresa's community, the Missionary Sisters of Charity.

Mathilde, Hadrien's girlfriend, tells us exactly where to go so that we don't waste time.

She is very nice and we become acquainted on the evening of our arrival in a bar in a doubtful alley.

The place, Chez Maria, is very informal with three tables, a hippie decor with music from the sixties and seventies. A haven of peace and love in the hubbub of the city.

Before going to Mother Teresa's, I have to hand over a book that a colleague gave me for one of her Indian friends.

I only have an address and a name. I leave Florence at our guest house and head off on my adventure. I want to try a rickshaw, these Indian tuk-tuks, which is the best way to get around here.

In Calcutta, at that period, there are still hand drivers. They carry the cart at arm's length and are barefoot.

But what to do? I know that this is a way for these people to earn their living.

I bargain for a price before embarking on this adventurous journey. I admit I feel ashamed as I climb in and sit on the seat.

The feeling I get is absolutely exhilarating, I think I'm flying over the street. I get an overview of all the stalls that go by from a height, and everything is typical, archaic for me.

I've never seen anything like it. I imagine shooting a film of colours and smells. I am the actress in a surrealist film, oh, how I love these feelings!

I learn that finding an address in India is not easy, most of the street names are not mentioned and you have to ask every five minutes in this urban jungle.

Finally, we are there and I am welcomed by Mira, my colleague's Indian friend.

She speaks French, because she studied it at Shanti Niketan, a university created by the Nobel Prize winner for literature, poet and humanist, Rabindranath Tagore.

I have a lot of fun in her presence. She is charming, educated and scholarly and caring. I feel as if I have known her all my life.

It is time for me to leave as the others are waiting for me, but I promise to keep in touch, which I will continue to do until today.

My *rickshaw wallah* is waiting for me and takes me back to the street where I live.

I had so much exhilaration from this unprecedented expedition, but also embarrassment from being hauled around like a maharani, that I tripled the amount he asked for.

The smile he gives me is the most beautiful gift I can receive.

It is unthinkable to leave without visiting the congregation of the Missionaries of Charity and visiting the tomb of Mother Teresa.

My *tuk-tuk* driver is on the street, and when he sees me, he looks ecstatic and rushes towards us.

- *Mother Teresa.*

He understands immediately and nods his head.

- *How much go Mother Teresa?*

I utter some gibberish so that he understands me.

- *No problem.*

"No problem" is the key word in India. Everyone will tell you "no problem", it's a philosophy here. There is never a problem and you will always find a solution, that's what it means.

The location of the community has nothing to do with the fame of the owner. Simple, quaint, but nevertheless moving.

Her tomb is enthroned in the middle of a large room in a minimalist simplicity.

A sister explains the work of the community to us, and we ask her if it is possible to visit one of the centres that receive children.

We were taken to a hospital for mentally handicapped children.

What a shock! We are in an indescribable state of unease. The mentally handicapped children are tied to the bars of their beds as they were at the beginning of the century in the orphanages.

There is a shortage of staff and some foreign sisters and volunteers are there and certainly are doing their best with the means available... But where does all the money that the missionaries of charity receive go to?

This is the question we ask ourselves as we leave, in addition to feeling immense sadness at the misery of the world and a deep sense of uneasiness.

On this mixed state of mind, we leave Calcutta, leaving Hadrien and Mathilde and promising to meet again in Switzerland.

We get to know Howrah, one of the three railway stations of the city, that is swarming with people, the sound goes up in the air, producing frightening and thundering echoes, and it seems to spread in all directions.

We are early and have to wait in this incessant uproar.

Many ragged children of all ages are begging, picking up newspapers thrown on the ground, garbage, bottles that they can recycle and whatever they can lay their hands on in order to make a few pennies.

These children of the station are notoriously known here. A man sitting next to us tells us to be careful of them, as they are thieves.

But what can we do before such distress and such encouraging smiles?

Two of them approach us, a boy and a girl. They are maybe seven or eight years old.

They hold out their hands and put them to their mouths, miming:

- I'm hungry, give me something to eat.

I try to make contact with them by smiling and gesturing:

- Do you speak English?
- M'am, food.

And they again mime the gesture of being hungry and show me the kiosk where you can buy food.

- Flo, I'm going with them to buy them something, can you look after our luggage?
- Yes, and you watch your money.

*

The children want chips and Coke, like all children in any part of the world.

They come back with me and sit down with us to quietly enjoy what I have just bought them.

The Indians around us look at us with an evil eye and our seatmate says with disdain in perfect English:

- They are thieves, dirty kids.

I smile at the man.

- Thank you, sir, goodbye, we've got to catch our train now.

- Have a nice trip, ladies, but be careful, you are in India.
- Thank you for the advice.

I feel safe on the contrary. The first few days spent here were most enjoyable and went off wonderfully well, so why shouldn't it continue?

The children accompany us to our car and say goodbye without having robbed us despite the predictions.

I can't help giving them a 100 rupee note, they are so irresistibly sweet... If I could, I would take them with me.

"Thank you, m'am, thank you, m'am."

Once again, it is their smile that remains in my mind and this simple happiness of surviving from day to day.

"Bye bye."

A little tear starts trickling at the edge of my eyes, I will never forget their faces.

We took second class tickets, not knowing Indian trains and their class categories.

We are seated on an uncomfortable bench and share the compartment with an Indian gentleman in his fifties.

We get to know each other and we talk a little about our lives. He is impressed to see two women travelling alone.

The journey will be long despite the short distance, he warns us, as the train stops often and we will only arrive at the break of dawn.

Luckily, we planned to buy sufficient provisions at the station, but above all we thought about water, because without drinking water we would either die of thirst or be down with some infections diarrhea that would have left us bedridden.

We share our picnic with Suresh, our travelling companion

who is also going to the same place as we are.

We fall asleep on our benches which serve as beds. We didn't think of taking a compartment with sleeping berths, so for want of anything better, we have to make some adjustments.

The rolling of the train gently lulls us to sleep. We fall into a restless sleep and even the numerous stops do not wake us up.

- "Hurry, hurry, wake up!" shouts Suresh, shaking us.

We are arriving in Puri.

We have no time to think and before we know it we are outside.

My eyes are burning with sleep and I struggle to open them wide as I climb onto the rickshaw that takes us to the guest house Suresh had recommended.

The day breaks and the not-yet-burning air that caresses my face gently wakes me up.

The early morning light is orange, enveloping me like arms that embrace me and welcome me.

The visuals that go past before my eyes invade my whole being. This luxuriant vegetation, these noises, these smells... Everything is just bursting with joy and I start floating with a smile on my face, with a sense of feeling so good in this moment.

Will I experience this feeling again? No one knows, so I take full advantage of this immeasurable joy.

The magic of India is undeniably working on me.

We stay for a week in Puri, in the state of Orissa, which is one of the seven holy cities of India and one of the four cities where Shankara founded a monastery of his monastic order, called Dashanami.

The city is entirely dedicated to Krishna and is one of the

holiest places of pilgrimage. But we Westerners, contrary to the Hindus, are not allowed to enter the temple.

Our guest house is near the beach. To get there, we have to pass through a fishing village. They live in huts covered with palm leaves.

We get acquainted with the children who ask us for pens and want to have their picture taken.

They always accompany us to the sea and tell us to be careful because the rolling waves are dangerous. We can only swim at the shore.

I want to immerse myself in the culture of Indian beauty and I decide to decorate my feet and hands by applying henna, *mehandi* in Hindi.

These designs are a form of protection and highlight the woman during different ceremonies such as weddings. They are very precise and intricate, full of symbols.

The beauty parlor is located on the ground floor of a village house. Nothing to do with the beauty salons I have been to in Paris. Rudimentary, but nice.

The beautician, who is tall for an Indian, is friendly and we communicate as best we can. She has a very limited knowledge of English, but somehow, we manage to communicate.

I stay for more than an hour so that she can finish her work, which is an art. At the end, she tells me that I have to keep the henna on for a maximum number of hours so that the colour is fixed on the skin.

I thus start walking around with my feet tucked inside plastic bags and my hands kept stiffly upright, unable to use them. A gypsy in the country of maharajas… but I look local.

Still a laughing stock, but what a handicap!

My girlfriend Flo falls for the local speciality, ganja, a narcotic herb sold freely in state-run shops.

She doesn't buy it, but one evening she orders a special lassi made of this hallucinogenic drug at the restaurant. We have a great evening laughing, but the she does not experience the expected symptoms according to her, and we go back to the guest house.

During the night she wakes me up with a start:
- Can you hear the hyenas outside?
- No, those are stray dogs.
- I tell you they are hyenas, we have to be careful and not go out.
- OK, go back to sleep.

Several hours later, once the digestion is over, the ganja started showing its full effect.

How we laughed at that story! We still do when we talk about it till today.

We enjoy this beautiful region to the fullest. Starting from local tribal cultures where we buy special handicrafts to the Konarak temple where we attend a recital of classical Odissi dance, everything is absolutely dazzling.

Our next stopover is New Delhi, where we arrive after more than a twenty-four-hour train journey but this time in a sleeping berth.

In front of me, I see a swarming and suffocating city, nothing to do with Bombay which has more open space, maybe thanks to the sea.

I start getting nausea, the first time since I came to India. I feel like vomiting and have a headache. I just want to go to bed. But we've yet to find a hotel.

Florence, who has been there before, directs us to the backpackers' district, Paharganj, where she has stayed before.

The guest house she knows is full. We have to find a place to stay quickly because my physical condition is getting worse and worse. I frequently have the urge to throw up and I am afraid of being ill on the streets.

We end up in a sleazy joint, the room has no windows, more a wardrobe than a room!

I rush to the toilet, emptying myself. I have to lie down. I immediately fall into a refreshing sleep. After this beneficial nap, I smile again and feel like my old self.

We have to look for a way to go to Dharamsala to see my Tibetan godson as we are nearing the end of the trip. We will conclude our vacation with this long-awaited visit that I was anxiously looking forward to.

New Delhi is hot, dusty, but attractive with an old-fashioned feeling where the English presence is still perceptible.

The main bazaar where we stay is full of shops where you can find everything a tourist wants to bring back home. The Indian Ali Baba's cave.

You are always being lured in to offer you anything and everything.

Indian fabrics, dishes, spices... and local travel agencies.

We let ourselves be taken in by one of them, I don't know how, and we end up on the first floor of a leather shop.

I explain to the man supposed to be the boss where we want to go. We start a tiresome bargaining over a cup of chai, or Indian tea.

After some tough negotiations, it is decided that we will go by car with a driver who will be at our disposal.

The appointment was finally scheduled very early the next morning, at the daybreak. It was the beginning of a nightmare, which is nevertheless funny looking back at it now.

It is six a.m. We are waiting for our driver as planned. At six thirty a.m., half an hour late, a minivan arrives with four men inside.

It can't be for us this car. I start to get impatient and start mumbling some unkind words.

The car stops in front of our hotel. A man gets out and asks for us in broken English.

I approach him.

- It's us, but why are all these men here?

And he starts blabbering a series of gibberish explaining that we are going to drop two of them in the city and that one of them is going to stay with us because the driver doesn't speak English and that he will act as translator.

It starts well, I let myself go and start shouting and of course he answers me with the inevitable Indian formula:

"No problem, Ma'am, no problem, Ma'am!"

What is there to say after their famous magic phrase of "no problem?" For them, there is never a problem.

I calm down because it is important for me to leave to see my young Tibetan.

The agency had informed us that the journey would last eight hours, so if we want to reach early in the evening, we have to hurry up and get started.

It takes us two hours to leave the city. First, we drop the two men in different places, which makes us lose time.

We are now on a kind of motorway. I don't trust the driver, I think he drives badly.

I'm not yet used to left-hand driving on the road and everything seems to be upside down. My friend is not very reassured either, especially when we see trucks crashed and overturned on the side of the road.

We drive on, we drive on, but I have the impression that we haven't made much progress. We've been driving for five hours already, and I ask:

- Where are we? Is it still far?

The two men look at each other and don't answer us.

- Is it still far?
- No, no, maybe five hours.

We are doubtful about their ignorance, twice they ask for directions, in fact they know nothing.

- Dharamsala, I shout in the driver's ear.
- Yes, yes no problem.

Flo tells me to drop it.

- They are stupid.

I need to take some fresh air to relax. I ask them to stop.

They take the opportunity to do their business. We see them leave in the thicket. Florence notices that they have left the key in the starter.

- We're going to scare the hell out of them, she says.

And she gets behind the wheel and starts up.

What a laugh! The two guys rush in, trousers still pulled down on their knees.

- No! no! Please! they shout.

We laugh until we cry and I tell them:

- No problem.

We're back on the main road once again. We get lost a thousand times, and a thousand times they ask for directions.

Fourteen hours since our departure, we are finally in Dharamsala.

We have to find a hotel without delay because it's in the middle of the night. I take matters into my own hands. I look in my guidebook for a place to sleep, and we weren't expecting it to be so cold outside.

We end up in the city's palace, or so-called palace, which only has the name. We got a room, that's the main thing.

We are exhausted. There is no heating, we are frozen. We are so drained out that we go to bed half dressed, we'll see about the rest tomorrow.

The next day we meet up with our companions waiting for us in the parking lot. We notice that they have slept in the car.

The poor buggers are freezing with their flip-flops on their feet. They had no idea where we were going and did not know that we would be at altitude.

We nevertheless feel sorry for them and offer them a cup of coffee. They accept without resentment, poor guys.

*

The TCV, Tibetan Children Village, is not in Dharamsala but in McLeod Ganj, where the Dalai Lama lives and which is about ten kilometres away, but we were unaware of that. The hotel receptionist tells us about this.

We arrive in this village where the atmosphere is really

Tibetan. The shops, the restaurants, a temple in the street... everything is Tibetan.

I shudder with ecstasy, I am home.

Traces of snow are still present and I have nothing to wear for this low temperature. I have to buy warm clothes, otherwise I won't last.

I enter the first shop I see. I find a cap and a Tibetan woolen blanket that I will use as a shawl. I'll take them back to Switzerland as a souvenir.

My friend laughs at seeing me dressed in this unsuitable outfit. I don't look like anything, perhaps like Alexandra David-Néel, the first French woman to enter Lhassa, the capital of Tibet.

I joke with her about my incongruous appearance.

- Ngawang Jampa will be scared when he sees me.

And we laugh even more.

The TCV is located still further above the village. Our two crazy Indian idiots take us up there and leave us at the entrance near the Dal Lake.

I am emotionally moved to seeing him, our first meeting... I am so anxious to discover him, to see him in reality.

We are greeted by the secretary who deals with the sponsorships of the Swiss association. She is a charming lady who explains a little about the children's lives and her work with the various organisations around the world.

I am nervous. They go to fetch him. We are waiting in the office and the difference in temperature with the outside is warming up my face. I'm all red, especially my nose.

I must look awful, far from the model I once was. Besides, the photos will prove it. I don't recognise myself in them. It is certainly the new Diane who appears on. It was such a powerful moment for me...

There he is, in front of me, the lady explains to him who I am. He doesn't understand English yet, communication is difficult.

He is so shy, that he doesn't dare to look at me. I am an alien for him. Certainly, the first western woman he sees.

What is going on in his head at this moment? I never really knew. When I asked him later on, he told me he didn't remember precisely his first moments together but that it was the best day of his life.

Me when I looked at him, I imagined with sadness this little boy crossing a whole country in the snow on foot, on truck, on horse to find freedom.

In any case now, I have the feeling that after such a long time, I am delicately touching with the tips of my fingers the life that I have been waiting for.

We ask him to show us around the village. He takes us all around the complex.

I understand that it is very well organised: a main square where important events and gatherings take place; all around, in the nature, houses that welcome refugee children and that are managed by Tibetan women who assume the role of mothers.

We are impressed by the love that reigns in all simplicity.

This first visit is undoubtedly short but this is only the beginning. I leave some money and the gifts I have brought for Ngawang Jampa.

I explain that I will come back and write to him.

I am sad to leave him, these few hours spent with him are just a taste of a beautiful story.

I am convinced of that.

I leave with a heavy heart but so happy to know that a young Tibetan is now part of my life.

*

The return to Delhi is as disastrous as when I first arrived there, but my head is lighter, full of memories of my entry into this Tibetan world which I had been fantasizing about since my teenage years.

This trip to India is already ending. I do my last shopping in the bazaar where I pick up my last souvenirs.

What an odyssey, quite unforgettable! Forever written in the book of my life.

On the return flight, I think of this first trip to India and my imaginary Tibet.

The only word that comes to mind is gorgeous. So many wonderful moments, sometimes funny, sad, moving, but by no means horrible... I can't wait to come back. I can't wait to see Ngawang Jampa again.

I am all in praise for India. I tell everyone about it. I have nothing but words of admiration when I talk about my Tibetan godson and the emotion always comes through in my voice.

I have to continue this connection with Buddhism that I started quite unknowingly by simply casually browsing through an article in a magazine.

There surely must be a Buddhist and Tibetan community in Switzerland.

One night while pondering over the matter, I have a flash of insight. I think of the Dalai Lama's teaching in France, which was organised by this French monastery, Karma Ling.

I'm going to phone them, they'll certainly be able to give me information.

They inform me that there is a monastery in the canton of Vaud, above Vevey, at Mont Pèlerin, what a lovely name! In fact, the association in Switzerland had told me about it but I had completely forgotten.

I have the soul of a pilgrim within me and keeping this in mind that I start visiting Rabten Choeling and the teachings of Gonsar Rinpoche at Mont Pélerin, a small village situated on the heights above Vevey by the Lake of Geneva.

It's quite small, well representative of the Tibetan culture with that spiritual atmosphere that I like so much.

I get to know the monks and nuns, both Tibetan and Western, who live there.

I go there every month to learn more about this philosophy, which is a conducting line guiding me through the path of life.

After two years of total impregnation, my lama master asks me, as if nothing had happened, during a conversation, if I would not like to take refuge.

My face surely reflects my ecstatic astonishment. I'm absolutely thrilled, I never thought he would suggest that to me.

- Do you think I am ready, Rinpoche?
- If I am suggesting it, then it's because I believe the time has come.

On a weekday chosen by Rinpoche, I become, in an intimate ceremony with two other participants, Lobsang Chökyi, which means: *an open mind that achieves something joyfully for the Dharma.*

The ordination ceremony in Buddhism is actually like a

baptism, we become Buddhists and take refuge in the Buddha, Dharma and Sangha. We are also initiated in the Buddhas, the teaching and the Buddhist community.

I am a Buddhist as of now.

To be part of this congregation, to have a Buddhist name, this is so precious to me... My childhood dream is coming true. But will I ever go to Tibet, in the footsteps of the Dalai Lama, to prostrate myself at the Potala, his residence? That's another chapter, but in any case, it was built in India, in McLeod Ganj and here, on Mont Pèlerin.

Yes, I am a Buddhist, yes, I am a Buddhist, my name is Lobsang Chökyi, I keep repeating in my head, smiling, after this consecration.

*

Several times a year, I receive a letter from the TCV telling me a little about Ngawang Jampa's life, his progress, the important moments and a word from him with always a drawing.

He draws superbly every time, I always look forward to seeing what he has conjured up. And I am still looking forward to this creative bond connecting our relationship a little more.

As of now I return to India every year, to see my godson but also to enjoy the country.

I have Indian friends in Delhi, Mumbai and Jaipur with whom I have a sincere friendship and whom I like to meet up with during my visits. They are like my landmarks, a bit like a family, and make me feel that I am a bit Indian and not totally a foreigner.

From time to time, India suddenly reminds me that I used to be a model. People on the street stop me to take my picture.

I don't know why they pick on me, because there are plenty of tourists, but they seem to be attracted to me.

When I first visit the Taj Mahal, I find myself more photographed than this prestigious monument. Entire families jostle to have me as a souvenir.

This reminiscence of my past amuses me. I pose, I smile, but I have this sense of fulfillment of being a complete person now.

Once, in Jaipur, my Indian friend who is also acting as my driver has to go to the garage to have the car we are travelling in checked.

It's hot and I step out to get a little more air, to breathe better. I sit on the edge of a wall.

Suddenly, all the workers present surround me and stare at me like a curious animal. They say they recognise me, that I am an American actress.

My driver laughs and plays up to that image. He tells them that we are going to the Jaisalmer desert to shoot a film.

I am amused, but I start asking myself, am I not still just a physical object for people?

I don't think so because I have evolved, but it is true that people only see the outside of me. Maybe I still have that lustful aura that I have had for years?

When I relate these anecdotes, people think I'm exaggerating, that I'm still living in a past that no longer exists for me. I let them believe what they want. I'm not hurt because deep down I know who I am.

On another occasion, I travel to India with a very close friend. We stay in a famous palace hotel in Mumbai.

The first time we go out on the streets, he can't believe his eyes. I'm mobbed to have my picture taken. Throughout our stay, it's like this. One day, he says to me, hilariously:

- It's not possible, they must think you're a porn queen!

I burst out laughing.

- It's true!

To this day, people still ask me to take my picture.

They like the colour of my hair, my style, my bearing and they always ask me if I am an actress.

A remnant of my past comes up every time. I automatically switch over to the former gait and carefully tutored swerves of the model I was once upon a time.

But I am aware of who I am, that my spirit has joined my body.

The glitter and glamour of the bygone days dazzle me while I pose for the photograph, but fade away to make room for the new Diane I have become, fulfilled and happy.

The relationship with my godson is growing each time and we enjoy each other's company, even if it is only for a short time in McLeod Ganj.

I don't send packages from Switzerland any more, but give him what he wants directly when I'm there and the little rascal knows exactly what he wants.

Nothing changes, always sports shoes, jeans and a little pocket money to have some fun with his friends.

He is now able to manage quite well in English, thus enabling us to communicate and interact better, which brings us a little closer.

His secondary school term is coming to an end and he now has to choose which direction he would like to take.

These young Tibetans are always pushed to continue their higher education and go as far as possible to get a good job.

The Swiss association through which I am sponsoring my

godson contacts me by phone and asks me what I plan to do next because he has to enroll in university.

The best thing is for me to call him and see what is best for him.

The new technologies that are now available to us make it easier to call each other and I do it right away.

He tells me that he has been accepted in Chennai, the former city of Madras, in the geography and tourism section.

He will need to pay school fees, accommodation and food and also have some pocket money at his disposal.

I suggest that it would be better if I sent him money every month, rather than going through the Swiss organisation.

He agrees, but I warn him that he will have to stay within his budget and manage his expenses properly, because I won't be able to provide any additional support.

A new and not so simple adventure begins for him, first leaving the cocoon of the children's village where he was protected, then being parachuted into another unknown universe without any protection net to cling on to.

A year after he moved to Chennai, I inform him of my arrival.

Meanwhile, along with a colleague, Joëlle, we founded an association, Surya Geneva, to help socio-cultural projects in India and we are currently sponsoring a home for street children in Pondicherry.

My annual trip will therefore take me to this region and I will automatically pass by Ngawang Jampa's house.

I'm looking forward to seeing where he lives and how he's managing on his own.

Finally, I am there. I am welcomed with open arms by him

and his roommates.

He shares a small flat with two young Tibetans, students like him, but in their second year.

They all decide that I will sleep there and not in a hotel. The camp members start making hasty arrangements, and one of them leaves me his "bed", well, actually his mattress, on the floor.

This is the first time I share a room with Ngawang. He is so proud that I am here!

I talk a lot with his friends, especially with Tenzin, who asks me about myself, my life and my investment for Tibet.

He opens up to me, tells me about his life and his love for his country and the Dalai Lama.

*

He makes me listen to Tibetan music and we interact with each other on Buddhist philosophy.

I spend three extraordinary days and my links with my godson imperceptibly tighten, as if it was predestined and written somewhere.

The day before my departure, I invite the entire group of people to a restaurant. These young people are unbelievable and their strength to take on life amazes me. They want to move ahead and that's a good sign.

In the evening, in the semi darkness, I talk to Ngawang Jampa:

- You know, I don't have any children and I consider you as the son I didn't have.
- So I can call you mummy, you have been taking care of

me for ten years, you are like my mother.

Tears of emotion run down my cheeks.

- Sleep well my son.
- You too, Mum.

Gradually, a parental bond has been forged over the years.
This is how Buddha gave me a son.

*

The second year of university is difficult for my son.

On the phone, I get the feeling he isn't doing that well. I absolutely must see what is going on.

This is my second visit to Chennai. When I see him, I realise that he is downright depressed. I ask him questions. I want to know a little more about his life. But he is so shy that it's hard to get to know him.

For him, everything is fine, he doesn't particularly like what he is doing, but everything is fine.

Tenzin, his roommate, tells me that my son has trouble with English because all the classes are in English and he is struggling with the lectures.

- It was the same for me, we have to persevere, and if you wish, we can discuss it together.
- Yes, thank you very much.

In the evening, during the dinner prepared by my son, who is a very good cook, Tenzin skillfully brings up the subject of studies.

- Jampa, your English is improving.

With a flushed face, he replies:

- Yes, it's much better.

I intervene by slipping in:
- You know, if you keep persevering, you'll get there, look at Tenzin, how well he speaks!
- Yes, Mum, I'll make it.
- I am confident because it is your future that is at stake.
- Yes, Mum, he says simply, without looking at me.

Tenzin looks serious.

You are lucky to have Diane who has never let you down and is looking after you, so don't let her down, she's your mother.
- Yes.

That's all he says.

The discussion is unproductive. It's closed and we won't get to know anything more.

What can I do? Nothing, it's his life.

The months go by, we call each other regularly. Of course, I ask about the university and his progress in English.
- Everything is fine, he says every time.

I trust him.

One day, I receive a letter from the TCV. I am surprised because I have not had any dealings with them since my son was in Chennai, apart for the New Year.

I'm flabbergasted with shock and almost fall of my chair when I read the letter.

I am told that Ngawang Jampa has not been attending university for three months and has therefore been written off.

This is not true, I don't believe it! He didn't tell me anything, according to him everything was fine.

He lied to me... But what is he doing then? What is he doing with the money I send him every month?

I discover at that moment what it means to be a Mother, its not all joy but also has its share of worries.

I look at the time to see if it's not too late with the time difference to call him. It's still possible.

- Hello, is everything all right?
- Yes, Mum.
- And at the university?
- Yes, everything is fine.
- Ngawang Jampa, I have received a letter and I know you have not been attending classes for months.

There is a silence, he says nothing. All I hear is the emptiness and his speechlessness.

I hang up in rage.

I'm upset, he lied to me. Why didn't he trust me?

I go back and forth over the last few years in my head. I'm trying to detect some signs. I want to understand, what have I done? Why did he leave the university?

It's true that it was difficult for him, that he wasn't really interested in the subjects he was learning.

But why not tell me about it?

I keep brooding over this subject until my head hurts and remember the days when I decided not to go back to school.

*

I hadn't mentioned anything to my mother or father because my parents wanted me to study. I was ashamed and was afraid of disappointing them.

With this problem, I have been thrust into my role as a Mother. He is afraid to confront me and to make me feel sad. I represent authority for him and his financial existence.

Poor guy, how upset he must be! I can't leave him feeling insecure and perhaps abandoned. He has already suffered enough in his life.

To be entrusted to a refugee smuggler and just dumped in an unfamiliar environment to fend for himself at the tender age of ten must be extremely shocking. To cross his country in the snow for three weeks in appalling conditions and arrive in a new country to survive in his own culture must be traumatic enough.

No, I really can't betray him. Our relationship is too strong and to deny what I have always wanted would be malicious and dishonest on my side.

I have to call him, set the record straight, tell him that I'm here for him, that I understand him and that we need to talk.

I hang up the phone now, my heart aching for what he told me and what I thought.

Abandonment, disappointment, unhappiness, to disappoint, Mother, leaving.

He doesn't like these classes which are useless to him. He doesn't want to disappoint me because I am the only person in his life, his mother.

He shyly tells me that he would like to go to Nepal, where his mother's sister is residing, and try to make a new life there.

What can I say but yes? I have to give him every chance to succeed, even if I don't agree on all the points.

He has to live his own life and it's not up to me to decide, I know what the situation is and I fall back on the example of my parents and their open-mindedness and positive education.

He leaves for Nepal the following month, I don't say anything but I am anxious about what will happen.

I wish him luck and ask him to give me news as soon as he

is settled.

I receive a letter some time later, telling me about his new existence.

He has been reunited with his aunt, the husband and his cousin who are putting him up at their place for the time being, and he has even found a job as a cook in a Tibetan restaurant.

He says he is happy.

Well, I'll go to Nepal to see him. I don't know this country, which is also the country of Buddha's birth when he was still Prince Siddhartha. What good reasons to go there!

He made this choice to live there and I hope that as an adult, he now takes on his own responsibilities.

I wait a few months for him to settle down in his new environment and then decide to have a chat with him.

- Babu, we need to talk.
- Yes, Mama.
- There you go, now that you're working and earning money, you're a man and I think it's time for you to stand on your own two feet.
- What does that mean, Mum?
- It means I won't be sending you any more money, but I'll always be there to help you if you have any problems. You have to manage your life now, like I told you, you're a man and you have to decide what you want to do.
- Yes, Mum.

All that he is able to utter is yes Mum, I think it's a shock for him to hear what I just said, but it was necessary, I repeat:

- I will never abandon you; you are my son.
- I love you, Mum.

That's it, the umbilical cord is slowly being cut, but it was necessary to do it.

Being assisted is not a life, you have to know how to let go of this safety net to move forward.

I am doing this for his own good, even if it will be difficult at first, he will understand later and thank me.

I still ask him if he needs anything, I can't help it. I need to cut the cord too.

- I'd like to take a cooking course. I want to become a professional.
- That's good Babu, that's a good idea. Find out the price and I'll send you the money.
- OK Mama, thank you.

Henceforth my son has taken charge of his life and I am proud of him. For more than a year he continues to be a cook and after finishing his training he finds a better job where he gets a higher salary.

I am reassured that he has found his path until he announces to me one day:

- Mama, I have found a job in a Tibetan monastery.
- That's great Babu, are you going to cook over there?
- No, I'm going to be an English teacher for the little monks.

And he tells me that he met a lama in charge of a monastery in Mustang who was looking for someone to teach English.

*

It was a well-paid job with board and lodging included, so I accepted. I will spend the winter in the plains and the summer in

the highlands at the monastery.
- But you don't want to be a cook any more, don't you like it?
- Yes, but it's better paid and quieter there.
- So go ahead Babu.

What can I say?

He is the master of his own destiny after all and I can only encourage him to improve his life.

*

Its been two years that I haven't seen my son. I decide to go to Nepal in April because he will have come down from the mountains. I miss him very much and I especially want to know what his life is like there.

He is waiting for me at the airport exit in Kathmandu and offers me the welcome *khata*.
- Babu, how happy I am to see you!
- Me too, Mama.

I find him glowing with health. On the way to the hotel, I ask him about his new life as he is not very talkative and I always have to keep probing him to extract any information.

He loves his new job and has discovered that he enjoys teaching these young monks.

He likes living at high altitude, it reminds him of Tibet and he can venture to the border of his native country which is very close.
- So life is good, all you need now is a wife.

He blushes. I like to tease him about it. It's true that I would like to be a Grandmother.

He booked me a hotel in the Buddhist quarter of Bodnath. It's beautiful, from my room I have a view of a huge stupa where people gather to walk around and meditate. I am delighted.

He suggests that I go and walk around it, which is called Kora.

I feel in communion with him in this spiritual journey, we make three turns because it must always be an odd number.

I am so happy to be with him again and to share these priceless moments with him!

In the evening, we are invited by his relatives, with whom he has been reunited. Unfortunately, his aunt passed away recently and he was not been able to get to know her well.

A very strong bond has been created with his cousin Paldon. She is married to Bikram and they live with his sister and mother. They have two children, a boy and a girl.

I am greeted as a member of the family and I am embarrassed when they thank me for what I have been doing for Ngawang Jampa.

While my son and Bikram's mother are in the kitchen preparing momos, similar to dumplings, I start chatting with him.

I come to know that he is a mountain guide and accompanies trekking groups to Mount Everest and other high-altitude camps.

He is a charming man; I have a lot of pleasure to confide in him about my life.

The exchange is fascinating and I learn a lot about Nepal with him.

The evening is delicious, and so is the food, a real family meal, and I am delighted to share this moment with all these lovely people.

Two days later we leave for Pokhara, where the monastery my son works for has set up its winter base.

The distance between Kathmandu and Pokhara is only 200 km, but the journey is endless.

The road is bad, closed in both directions in some places, and we have to wait for our turn to go by, not just ten minutes but sometimes forty-five.

Finally, we arrive after eight hours on the road. I am exhausted.

The scenery is magnificent: a lake and, as a backdrop, the Annapurna peak.

I stay in a very cute hotel run by Tibetans, but the problem is that I have to juggle with the electricity schedule, because every day there are power cuts at random and at different times.

At certain times, there is no wi-fi, no television, back to the stone age, but you soon get used to it.

The week here is enjoyable to the fullest. We walk around, we laugh, we fight over small trifles, time stands still and I use every precious moment to make the most of my son's presence.

He introduces me to his job, to the lama director and to the students. Everyone surrounds me, respects me, thanks me once again for my deeds.

Ngawang Jampa introduces me as his mother and some of the little monks ask why we don't resemble each other, saying that he is tanned and I am completely white. We find it so funny!

We have become very close, as we have never been before, just like a true Mother and son relationship.

I'm so happy to have reached this point!

Life finally gave me the child I wanted, and as fate would have it, Ngawang Jampa was born the same year I lost the child

I was expecting from the man of my life.

*

Our relationship is sincere and unambiguous. The bonds we have built up over the years have been consolidated and confirmed.

Lord Buddha actually gave me a son, I would even say offered it, and what's more, from Tibet, a country that has always attracted and bewitched me.

I leave Nepal with a light heart, full of wonderful memories with my son, his family, his friends, his new life over here. I am reassured to know that he is in good hands and that he is happy.

I promise to come back next year and whisper to him as I proceed to leave him at the airport:
- You know, I'd love to be a Grandmother.

He smiles at me, his face flushed, but says nothing.

As promised, I come back the next year, then another year, and to my surprise, my son tells me he is in love and wants to get married.

My heart leapt with joy, I thought it would never happen!
- Babu, how wonderful! Tell me, who is she?

And he tells me in his own way, shyly, the story of how they met.
- She is from Mustang, a new teacher at the monastery, and already shares his life.

He is happy, he tells me.

I'm happy too, and we talk about wedding preparations.

I go back to Switzerland with this beautiful project in mind: to get my son married.

Every time we call each other, we talk about marriage. I start putting a bit of pressure on him because I have to make arrangements in advance.

After all, I'm the groom's mother, I have to help him, it's my role and I want to do it.

It's a bit complicated to find a date that suits everyone, but finally, after many changes, the month of December has been fixed.

I plan to go there for three weeks to organise the ceremony with them, before, during and after.

I consider it my duty to be present throughout the preparations because he only has me and I will also represent his family from Tibet, especially his mother, whom I do not forget.

The auspicious date of 8th of December has been finalized.

On my arrival, I am greeted as usual by my son, but this time his fiancée is with him.

Both of them offer me the welcome scarf. She is very shy and doesn't dare make eye contact with me. I try to put her at ease by talking to her, asking her questions, but it is still difficult for her.

I put myself in her shoes and understand her. I remember how cold Yannis' parents were towards me and how they didn't like me.

I don't want them to go through what I suffered, as I don't feel the need to be a nasty mother-in-law, but rather a loving and warm-hearted person.

I'm so happy that my son has finally found a suitable match and moreover, this young woman is really charming!

A new kind of feeling, that is very strong and overpowering, comes over me and makes me realise how far I have gone through the path of my spiritual life, in my Buddhist philosophy. Today, being a Mother takes on a new, intense, vibrant, different taste for me.

I discover that I am more maternal, more involved, more proud.

While driving in the car on our way to the hotel, she doesn't utter a word but I sense she is caring towards me.

It was she who found this guest house where one of her school friends works. I had expressed the wish to have a kitchen to do my own cooking.

I am delighted with this charming little flat, with a bedroom, a kitchen, a bathroom and a living room, absolutely ideal and perfect for me.

Soon I will be a mother-in-law. Who would have thought that would ever happen to me?

The wedding is in three days, so we're hastily making the final arrangements. Nothing has to be forgotten or missed out.

The bride and groom's traditional outfits are still at the tailor's. We'll have to pick them up the day before. My outfit will consist of a black sequined tunic that I got tailored in India with a long mouse grey muslin skirt.

I would like to take part in the preparations and express my desire to do so, for they don't want me to get tired.

- Babu, I am your mother and I have to help; besides, I am getting bored sitting in the guest house all day long.

- OK, Mama.

I am like a fish in water in my role as Mother of the groom. I give my opinion on everything. I want everything to be perfect.

Deep down inside, there is a certain sadness that is palpable.

My own marriage ceremony to Yannis is very much present, well, my marriage... or rather his burial.

The end of a dream, the beginning of a story, a family. Yannis, me and the loss of our unborn child, it all crumbled down in a few seconds. The end of a life that had barely begun.

My son doesn't know my story and I won't spoil his happiness with my sorrow. It's my business, it belongs to me, hidden in the depths of my heart in a cruel space of my life.

Today, the day before the wedding, we go to the banquet hall that has been rented.

The owner, on seeing me, is taken aback when my son tells him that I am his mother.

As a result, everything is easier and we become VIPs.

The place is really spacious, and it's for us to transform it into a wedding hall for the next day.

There has to be a platform where the bride and groom and their close friends and family will be seated. The father of the bride, one of the sisters and myself will be there, surrounded by devotional Buddhist decorations and auspicious protections.

A friend of my son's whom I know will be the mistress of ceremony. She asks me to give a speech on the day of the ceremony.

I start panicking, I don't dare do it, but she tells me it's important, that I'm the Mother and it's the custom.

It's true, I can't really back out, but I'll prepare exactly what I want to say.

Now I only have my speech in mind. What should I say? It has to be intelligent and understandable, and I first need to draft it in French and then in English and have it corrected. It has to be perfect.

The ideas start flowing in gradually. After that I will need to unfold the complexity of my thoughts as in a puzzle.

It's getting late and my son notices that I'm feeling tired.

- Mum, you can go back to the hotel, we'll finish everything tonight and it will be late for you. You must get some rest for tomorrow.
- You are right, Babu, it's better I make a move.
- He calls a taxi that will also pick me up the next day.

My mind wanders from Athens to Kathmandu in the car, all the way from Athens to Kathmandu in this perpetual quest for serenity, for Buddhist wisdom.

In my room, I write my text, once, twice, I start again and finalize it, I am satisfied with the results:

Il y a plus de vingt ans, j'ai parrainé un jeune tibétain du nom de Ngawang Jampa au TCV à Dharamsala.

Tout de suite, nous avons eu une vraie connexion et depuis ce jour, nous sommes devenus de plus en plus proches, comme mére et son fils.

Je remercie Lord Bouddha et le Tibet qui m'ont donné un fils comme lui.

Je suis tellement heureuse aujourd'hui et très fière d'être là, au mariage de Jampa et Pema.

J'aimerais partager ce moment heureux avec sa mère et sa famille au Tibet ainsi que vous tous ici.

Je souhaite à mon fils chéri et sa femme Pema une vie pleine de lumière, d'amour, de succès et de bonheur.

Love you.

This was the text I drafted in French. Once translated into English, I send it to Nadia, my very close friend in Mumbai.

She promptly returns the corrected version to me, with just a minor change in the wording of a sentence.

It came straight out of my heart, from my mother's soul, that the words just flowed into my mind without difficulty.

I just had to put my thoughts in order.

I go to bed peacefully, with a sense of utmost fulfillment. The night is nevertheless disturbed by dreams that mix the past and the present.

I wake up a little stressed. I must be ready on time, beautiful and bright for him, for them, for me.

Today is a big day, it is my son's wedding.

Thank you, Lord Buddha, for giving me a son.

I am picked up by car and afterwards we have to pick up the school's lama and a Swiss lady who is sponsoring the monastery.

I find myself looking particularly radiant beautiful, all proud to be marrying my son.

I am greeted at the entrance of the reception hall by friends of my son. A ritual of blessing will be required on my behalf and they brief me on how to perform it, after which I enter the banquet hall.

How beautifully it has been transformed into a real Tibetan wedding!

The bride and groom follow me, my son enters first and prostrates himself before the Buddhist altar.

Normally a photo of His Holiness the Dalai Lama should have been displayed there, but as these photos will be sent to his family residing in Tibet, it would put them into trouble if the Chinese intercepted the mail, which is indeed very sad.

The bride-to-be enters, they seat themselves on the wedding chairs placed on the platform, and then it's me. Oh my, how impressed I am! Then it's the bride's father's turn followed by one of the sisters.

I sit on the left side of my son and represent his only family. I think of his real mother and I am moved. I will represent her with dignity during this ceremony and deep down I thank her for giving me the chance to live these precious moments.

Everything is well organised and the mistress of ceremony is absolutely perfect. A snack is offered and once all the guests have arrived, the speeches begin.

Each guest talks about his/her relationship with the newlyweds, wishes them all the best and gives them advice on life.

Once again, I am thanked for my investment in my son. An uncle of the bride, who seems to enjoy talking, makes a never-ending speech that just drags on, addressing the groom in particular:

- Your mother, this woman from abroad who supported you throughout your life, you must, when she is old, help her in your turn and take her with you. A son should do this for his parents.

I see a moved expression on Babu's face and he nods as he looks at me. A current of love flows between us.

Then it is my turn:

I am deeply moved, excuse my English, I am going to read because I am afraid to stammer:

It's been more than twenty years that I met a young boy called Ngawang Jampa at TCV in Dharamsala.

We instantly connected and since that day to today we have become more and more closer as a Mother and a son.

I thank Lord Buddha and Tibet that they gave me a son like Ngawang Jampa.

I am so happy today and immensely proud to be part of Jampa's marriage with Pema and also to share this happy moment with his mum and family in Tibet and with all of you here.

I wish to my beloved son and his wife Pema a life full of lights, success and happiness.

Love you.

And I burst into tears.

I take my son in my arms, hug him tightly and kiss him and wife who is so sweet.

Everyone claps.

After all these good wishes comes the moment of exchanging the rings. Prayers and incantations are said by monks in front of the altar and then I receive the rings and pass them to my son. He puts the blessed ring on his future wife, then it's her turn to do so.

They are married. I now have a daughter-in-law who calls me Mother.

Now all the guests pass before us and offer us a *khata*, the scarf of bliss, as well as an envelope of wishes for happiness, some with a cash gift inside.

I end up with about fifty scarves piled up on me, but these gestures of thanks and protection delight me, it's very symbolic and it's an essential Buddhist ritual.

A buffet is served with delicious Indian food with an additional plus point for me, because it's not spicy. It goes without saying that both Tibetans and Nepalese cannot visualise eating food without chilies and not just a little bit!

The evening continues with songs sung by the guests and folk dances. Everyone participates in their own way in a pleasant atmosphere.

I start getting acquainted with the guests who are either friends or relatives of the new bride.

I feel good in my role as a Mother and on this beautiful day I feel peaceful with my emotions and in my heart.

I dance, I have fun, I enjoy these enchanting moments and I retain them in my memory to tell them later to my grandchildren, who I hope will soon arrive.

Everything is going wonderfully well; the people are happy and so are the bride and groom. The wedding along with the ceremony were more than successful.

Fatigue soon starts catching up with me and I see my son looking at me.

He comes to me straight away.
- Mama, do you want to go back to the hotel?
- Yes Babu, I think that would be more reasonable.
- I'll order a taxi for you.

*

Everyone greets me, the owner of the hotel wants a feedback from me and asks me if I am happy and wants to take a photo with me. My opinion is of great importance, so I reassure him and tell him that everything was perfect.

The taxi arrives and I step in.

The journey is short but the memories of this beautiful day are still lingering in my mind, when the dream of my life came true.

I am a Mother, I have a son, a daughter-in-law, all that is lacking are now grandchildren.

Buddha really gave me a son. Thank you.

The next few days are punctuated by visits from my son and his wife, meals in restaurants to thank each other and the family.

I had a crush on Pema's father, a widower. My daughter-in-law lost her mother at a very young age.

He specially came down from Mustang to attend the wedding and a kind of chemistry happened between us, I don't know how, because the language barrier made it impossible to communicate.

We looked at each other and understood each other. The love we have for our children is certainly a common language.

I am feeling cold in my hotel because there is no heating, and even the small electric heater I purchased is not sufficient to warm me up, and I end up falling sick.

My daughter-in-law is worried and asks my son to come and cook for me because I can't go out. I have to stay warm so I don't have a relapse.

He comes in the morning to make my lunch, and then both of them come back around five p.m. after work for dinner.

My son is effectively implementing his cooking skills and prepares delicious dishes for me which we all enjoy together.

A real family life.

But this kind of lifestyle where I'm sitting idle and helpless doesn't satisfy me. I decide to leave earlier. What's the point of them having to come and look after me?

I never liked being a burden to anyone.

I call the airline I with which I had flown earlier to find out if I can change my ticket, but more importantly to find out the price. Everything was arranged without any problems.

The next day, I go to the agency with my son and, for an extra charge of 50 euros, I can take the return flight back home.

I will leave two days later because there are no flights every day.

On the day of my departure, my children are there, everyone is sad.

With a heavy heart I say goodbye to Babu in tears. He gives me a big hug and I tell him I love him. His wife is also crying. I hug them and wish them all the best and express my love to them.

I don't want them to accompany me to the airport, that would make it more unbearable.

Before getting into the taxi, they give me scarves and wish me a good trip, we cry with emotion.

I am sad to leave them, but at the same time I am serene. I have succeeded one part of my life. I have a son whom I have just married, a Tibetan son, of the culture and philosophy I have always revered. I am fully in agreement with myself in this choice of my life.

I truly have a son that Buddha offered me.

I return home with a heavy heart at the thought of leaving them all behind but full of happiness after what I have just experienced.

Epilogue

I am back to my life which is now in France. The holiday season is coming up with all its preparations.

I relate this beautiful experience of the wedding to my family and friends and I am proud to have gone through with my convictions and my dreams.

But as I tell my story, I have the impression that something is missing. But what?

I keep it in the back of my mind, the universe will give me the answer one day.

I'm flying to London with friends for New Year's Eve and I'm planning to have fun like a teenager. I have to admit that I have always loved this city and my life with Yannis here was so sweet...

Despite a wistful nostalgia, I am fine. The wounds have been sealed but not healed and my love story will always be engraved within me in every drop of blood, anchored deep inside me.

I think he was my one and only passion, the others I experienced were merely meaningless replicas, without any depth.

On New Year's Eve, Yannis appears in my dream and speaks to me.

- Little girl, you must adopt this child you have. Our story is not over and we will meet again, we will continue what we had started. I love you.

I wake up sweating and confused, this dream was so real that I am totally shaken.

Adopt Babu, yes, it makes sense because I have to finish what had been started and officialize the relationship.

I send a message to my son expressing my desire, asking for his opinion and particularly if he would agree. We had never talked about this before and he had never asked me, so I am anxious to know.

His answer is loud and clear:

- I agree with you from the bottom of my heart, Mum. For more than half of my life, you've taken care of me and looked after me. To be honest, I love you more than my biological mother. I am so happy that you had the lovely thought to adopt me! I am your son forever. I love you mum.

Yannis was right and from where he is, he saw what was missing in my life. I am moved, terribly moved by my son's message. And to top up this beautiful story, that he will also become my legal son.

I make all the enquiries relating to adoption formalities. I get to know that it will be a simple adoption because he is too old for a full adoption.

He will be able to add my name to his, will be on my family record book and will be my heir. He will be able to apply for French nationality later on but will not automatically obtain it.

For me, this is a very symbolic and essential step in my life.

I need to find a lawyer because the process is a bit complex and I can't handle it alone.

But it's not easy to find the right person. I start making enquiries among my acquaintances. I hit upon two who seem more interested in money than in my case.

In the end, it's my friend Mireille, who has been living in France since her retirement, who finds me the rare gem.

Without hesitating I make an appointment straight away.

A week later, I land in her office, and we immediately get along very well.

I explain the situation to her, showed her photos, and relate a few stories about my relationship with my son.

When I mention certain Mother/child issues, I have tears in my eyes, but I can see that she also gets emotional.

She understands everything, values the importance of wanting to adopt my son and tells me that it is a wonderful story.

Everything is perfect with her, her listening, her professionalism, her kindness. Thank you.

I have to gather witnesses from third parties who were aware of this episode in my life and then register the simple adoption with a notary and have it validated by the court.

The procedure will go through the French embassy in Kathmandu where my son's wish to be adopted will be ratified and granted.

I leave there with a smile on my face and a heart full of joy.

I immediately inform my son by phone about this:

- Babu, I've just come from the lawyer's office, I'm starting the adoption procedures for you.
- Oh, that's great, Mum.
- Babu, she needs a copy of your identity card.
- I'll see what I can do because mine is not up to date.
- Okay, but do it quickly.

Weeks go by and I have no more news about this identity

card. I get irritated and tell him that if I don't have the card within a month, I'll won't proceed any further.

Nothing happens, no sign of any documents in the horizon.

In the end, it was his wife, whom I spoke to on the phone one day, who told me that one certificate was missing and that it could only be obtained in India.

I understand, but why doesn't he tell me about it himself?

Sometime later, he informs me himself that he will go in October, during his holidays, to get the missing document.

He couldn't go earlier because of his new job.

It's so much easier to tell the truth… but he still doesn't feel comfortable with me. He is afraid I will scold him.

A real Mother/child relationship.

So I wait and inform my lawyer about the delay.

As fate would have it, I chose her, she is such an understanding woman and I see in her a real empathy!

- Good morning, Madame, thank you for this information. Seeing that I am anxious, she tells me not to worry.

What generosity! I'm reassured and I'll wait patiently.

I am finally reaching the end of a dream and I don't want it to slip through my fingers. The hope of a lifetime that could just vanish into thin air… I am afraid.

I have to overcome these obstacles and meditation helps me not to make a mountain out of a molehill and see the positive side of things. It gives me great inner support and calms my agitated mind.

I am now able to soothe the film of my thoughts that is being screened before me and to find a certain gentleness by letting them go by without capturing any of them. This was no easy task but thanks to years of practice, I have been able to master this technique.

I patiently allow time to pass by meeting friends and following the course of my present life.

October is here, my son calls me:
- Mum, I have the certificate and as soon as I come back I can make my identity card.
- Babu, that's wonderful! I will inform my lawyer straight away.

From now on, nothing can stop me from really believing it. We're getting there, we're finalizing this simple adoption.

Things start moving one after another now. My lawyer is of an incredible efficiency, all the documents are ready, as well as the notary in France where I will sign my application, the French embassy in Nepal where my son will testify and give his consent, the high court in Marseille.

I am now officially Ngawang Jampa's mother. He appears in my family records booklet as my son and bears my name.

The apotheosis of a whole life, thank you Buddha, thank you Universe.

Thank you, Babu, for existing, for having come as a toddler into my life and grown up in course of time, and for treading on my steps so that they become one on the path of our common lives.

He is happy too. We will celebrate this joy together when I go to Nepal soon to visit him.

We will have a party with his wife and the whole Tibetan and Nepalese family to commemorate a Mother's love for her son.

I am glowing with joy and sharing my happiness with

everyone. If only Yannis were here…

One day during a holiday at my brotherly friend Roger's house, the discussion comes up about my life with Yannis, and how fate made it impossible for me to marry him.

Everything was ready, but death came slyly and destroyed everything, taking with it, the day before our wedding, the man I loved and our child.

I was so keen on becoming his wife before the Lord.

Its while going through these sad reflections that a smile appears on Roger's lips.

- You know I have an idea…
- Ah, what is it?
- You know I told you about that French Orthodox priest I met at a friend's house.
- Yes, I remember him vaguely, but isn't he French?
- Yes, French, a former fashion photographer turned pope. Let me call him and tell him your story. It would be so great if he could marry you posthumously!

It brings tears to my eyes.

- Another dream that could come true, I say, crying softly like a little girl.
- Leave it to me and I'll let you know.
- Thank you, I love you dear brother.

I put the idea aside, not wanting to get too excited.

- Hello Diane darling?
- Roger, how are you?
- Good, very good. Can you guess?
- Are you in love?
- Well, that's for sure, you know me and this time I think I've found the right person, but that's not what I want to talk

about.
- Tell me then.
- The orthodox priest, I told him about you, about your history and he even remembers having known you during your modeling days!
- I see! But that was a long time ago. So what happened?
- Well, he agrees to perform a wedding blessing ceremony, even if it's not very Catholic, or I should rather say Orthodox! My brother says, laughing.
- It's not possible, it's not possible… I don't know what to say.
- So, are you still keen on the idea?
- Oh yes, of course.

One Sunday, secretly, in an Orthodox chapel in France and surrounded by very close friends, the Pope blesses me and consecrates my union with Yannis.

I can feel it vibrating inside me, we are finally married.

The circle is complete, marriage with the man I love, a son. I am radiant and overjoyed.

One summer evening, destiny knocks on my door once again. It's true that Yannis is so present that I haven't really managed to start my life again.

During a fancy-dress party at a friend's house in a beautiful castle in the South of France, a man dressed as an angel approaches me and asks if he can sit down.

It leads to a discussion about us and our lives.

We are totally engrossed in a bubble, we don't pay attention to others.

A compelling need to reveal ourselves makes us get carried

away. We are alone in the world, as in a dream, a special kind of dream because we never met before. It is magical.

I have to leave, my friends with whom I came are pushing me to go home with them, but I feel so elated with the Angel that I would like to stay and talk with him for many more nights to come.

I'm sitting in the car on the way back, and my friends are pressing me with questions.

- Who is this Angel, Diane? You were both so absorbed in each other in a universe that we couldn't enter, that we couldn't even approach.
- I don't know who he is, and neither do I know his name, he's the Angel to me.
- What an incredible story!
- Yes, supernatural. And today is the 6th of July, the date of my meeting with Yannis in Greece.

THE END